BB WOLF
— AND THE —
THREE LPs

BB WOLF
— AND THE —
THREE LPs

JD Arnold &
Rich Koslowski

Top Shelf Productions
Atlanta / Portland

ISBN 978-1-60309-029-2

1. Fairy Tales
2. Blues Music
3. Graphic Novels

BB Wolf and the 3 LPs © 2010 Johnnie
Arnold and Rich Koslowski. Cover
design by Troy Geddes. Art direction
by Brett Warnock. Lettering by
Tony Guaraldi-Brown. Thanks to C.J.
Bettin and Chrissy Schuster for book
assembly edits and assists. Published
by Top Shelf Productions, PO Box
1282, Marietta, GA 30061-1282, USA.
Publishers: Brett Warnock and Chris
Staros. Top Shelf Productions® and
the Top Shelf logo are registered
trademarks of Top Shelf Productions,
Inc. All Rights Reserved. No part of this
publication may be reproduced without
permission, except for small excerpts
for purposes of review. Paper texture
backgrounds from Naldz Graphics.
Wolfram font copyright 2010 by The
Scriptorium, all rights reserved. Visit
our online catalog at www.topshelfcomix.
com. First Printing, May 2010.
Printed in China.

Dedicated to the memory of Emmett Till
and the countless lives cut short in the struggle for equality.
—JD

Don't leave home, there's nothing
but starving wolves outside.
—Inmemory, *Our House of Straw*

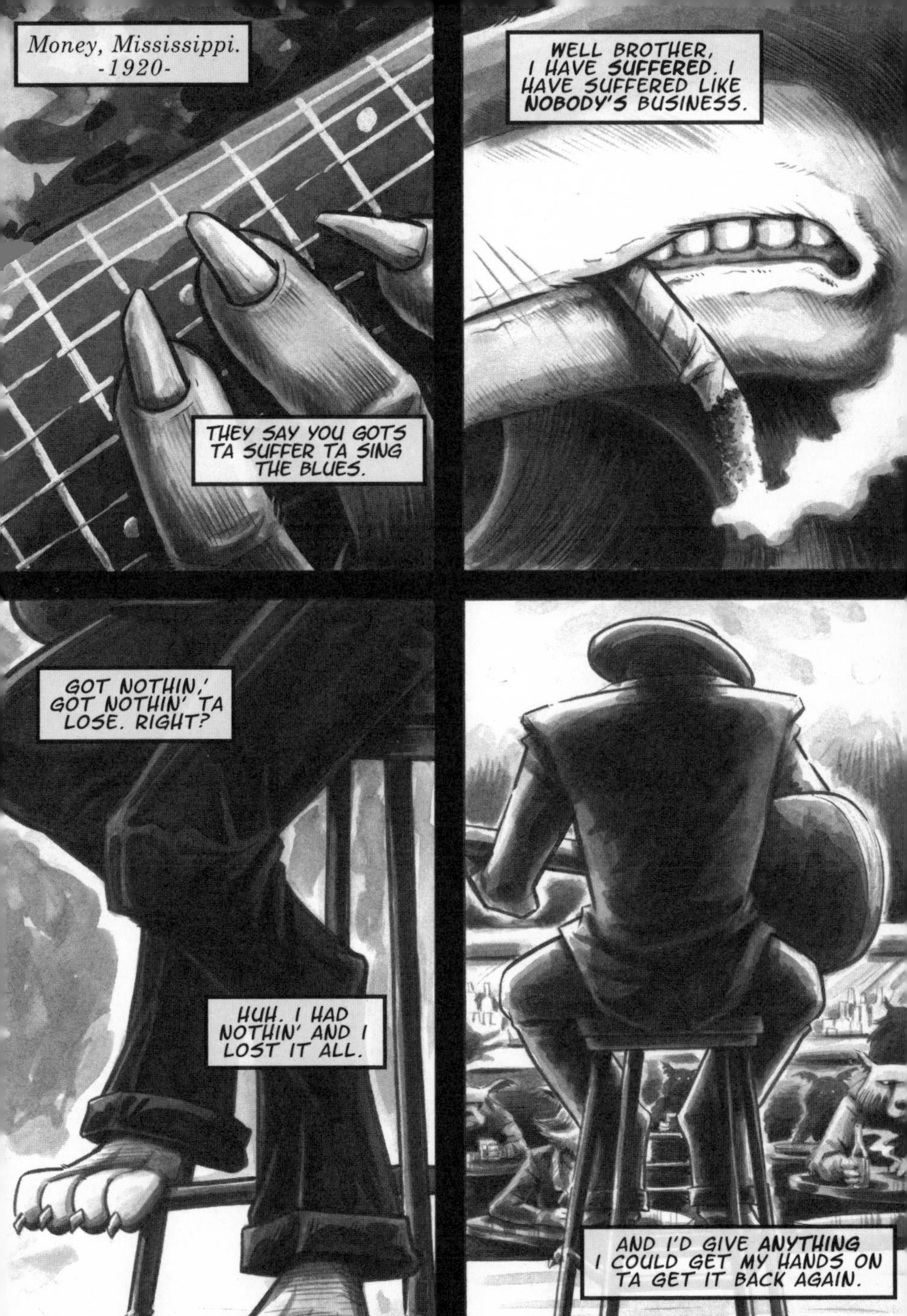
Money, Mississippi.
-1920-
THEY SAY YOU GOTS TA SUFFER TA SING THE BLUES.
WELL BROTHER, I HAVE SUFFERED. I HAVE SUFFERED LIKE NOBODY'S BUSINESS.
GOT NOTHIN,' GOT NOTHIN' TA LOSE. RIGHT?
HUH. I HAD NOTHIN' AND I LOST IT ALL.
AND I'D GIVE ANYTHING I COULD GET MY HANDS ON TA GET IT BACK AGAIN.

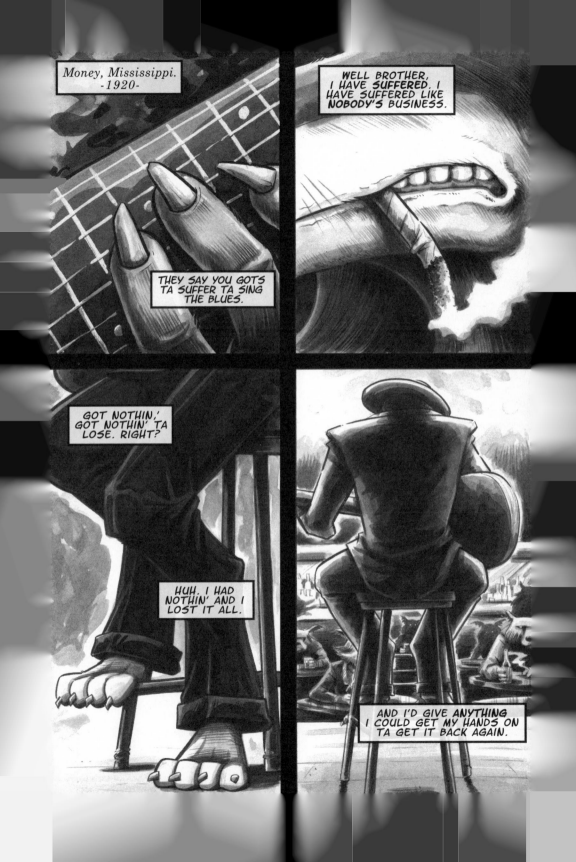

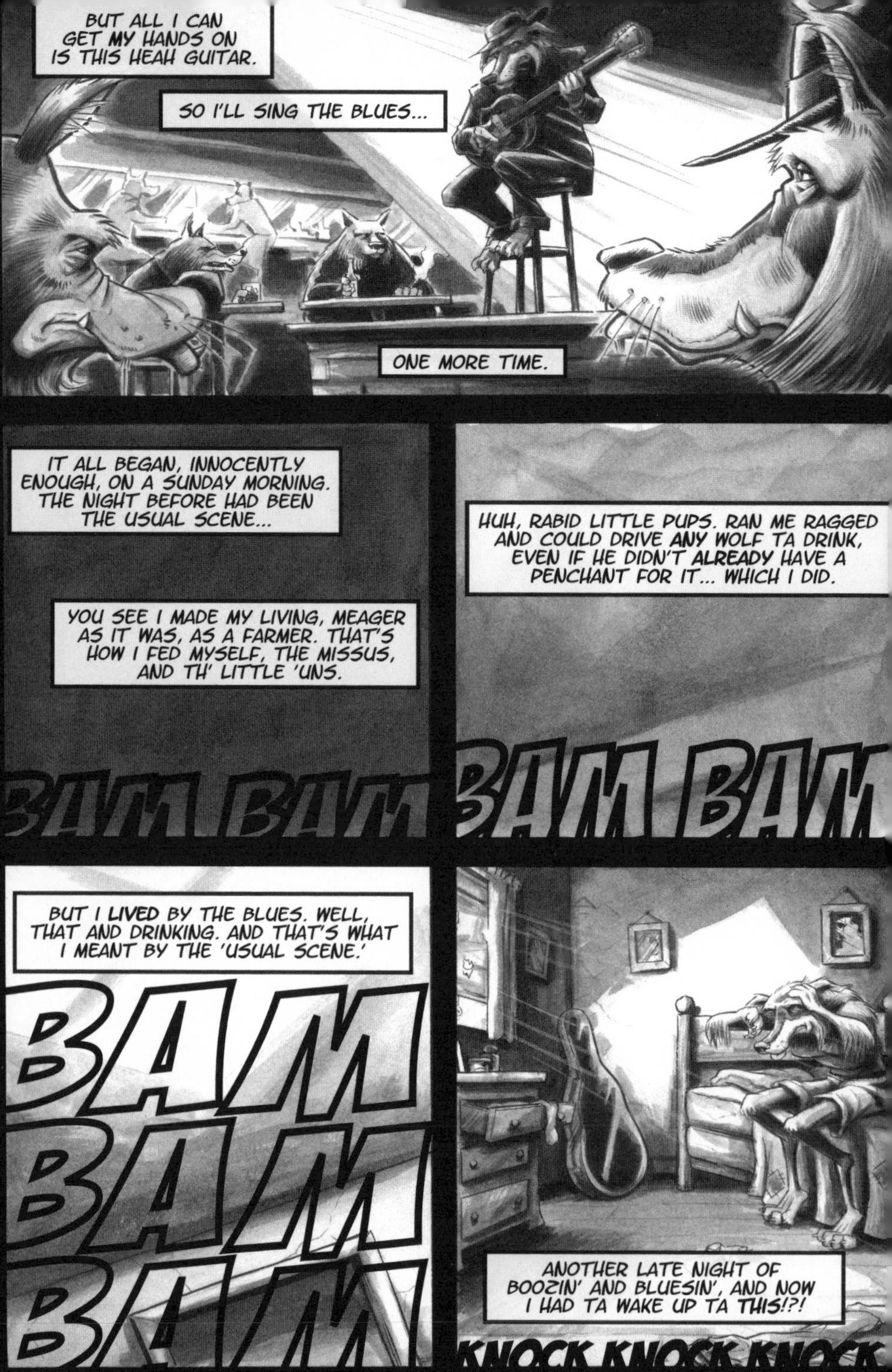
BUT ALL I CAN GET MY HANDS ON IS THIS HEAH GUITAR.
SO I'LL SING THE BLUES...
ONE MORE TIME.
IT ALL BEGAN, INNOCENTLY ENOUGH, ON A SUNDAY MORNING. THE NIGHT BEFORE HAD BEEN THE USUAL SCENE...
YOU SEE I MADE MY LIVING, MEAGER AS IT WAS, AS A FARMER. THAT'S HOW I FED MYSELF, THE MISSUS, AND TH' LITTLE 'UNS.
HUH, RABID LITTLE PUPS. RAN ME RAGGED AND COULD DRIVE ANY WOLF TA DRINK, EVEN IF HE DIDN'T ALREADY HAVE A PENCHANT FOR IT... WHICH I DID.
BAM BAM BAM BAM
BUT I LIVED BY THE BLUES. WELL, THAT AND DRINKING. AND THAT'S WHAT I MEANT BY THE 'USUAL SCENE.'
BAM
BAM
BAM
ANOTHER LATE NIGHT OF BOOZIN' AND BLUESIN', AND NOW I HAD TA WAKE UP TA THIS!?!
KNOCK KNOCK KNOCK

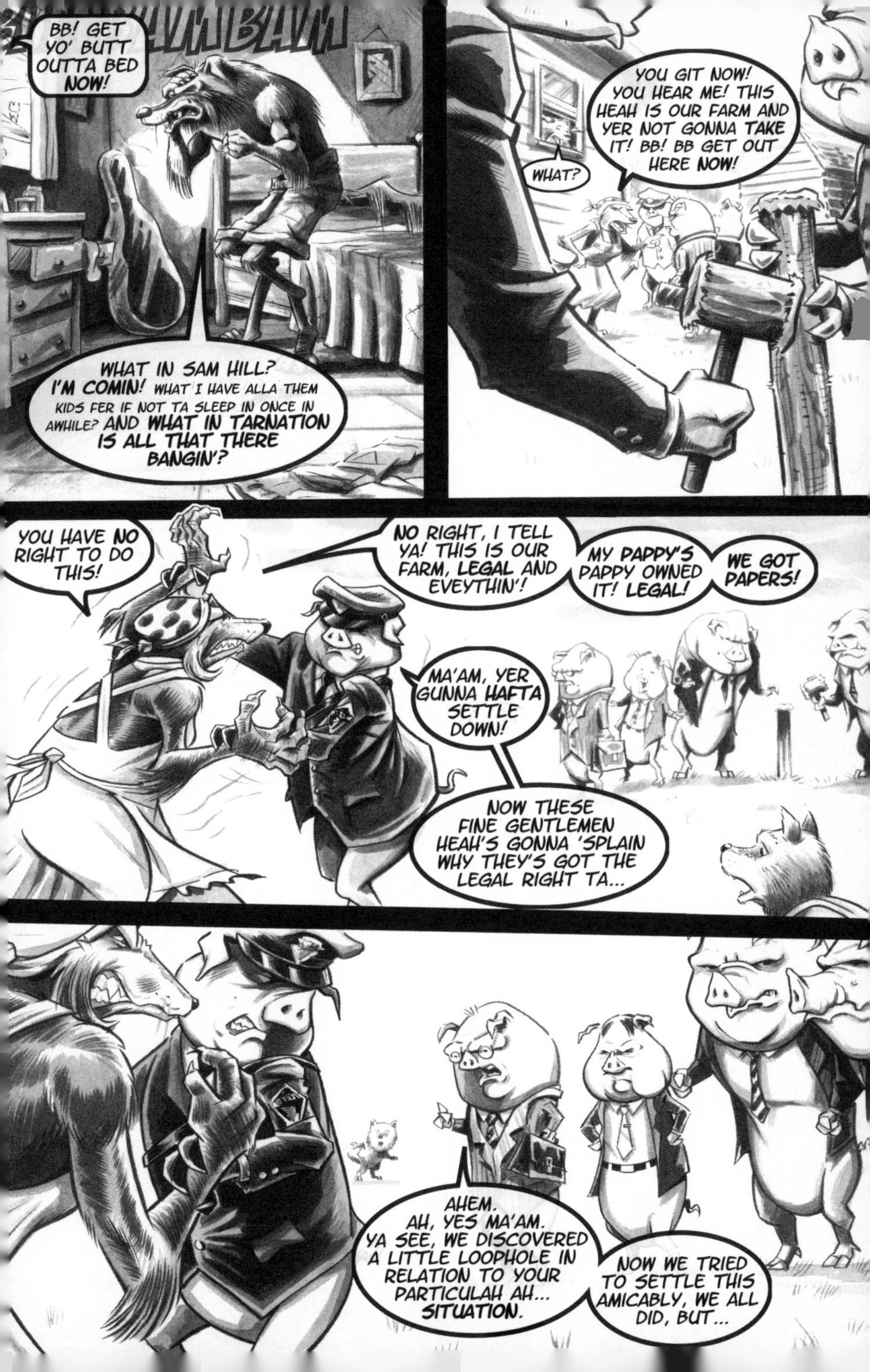
BB! GET YO' BUTT OUTTA BED NOW!
WHAT IN SAM HILL? I'M COMIN! WHAT I HAVE ALLA THEM KIDS FER IF NOT TA SLEEP IN ONCE IN AWHILE? AND WHAT IN TARNATION IS ALL THAT THERE BANGIN'?
WHAT?
YOU GIT NOW! YOU HEAR ME! THIS HEAH IS OUR FARM AND YER NOT GONNA TAKE IT! BB! BB GET OUT HERE NOW!
YOU HAVE NO RIGHT TO DO THIS!
NO RIGHT, I TELL YA! THIS IS OUR FARM, LEGAL AND EVEYTHIN'!
MY PAPPY'S PAPPY OWNED IT! LEGAL!
WE GOT PAPERS!
MA'AM, YER GUNNA HAFTA SETTLE DOWN!
NOW THESE FINE GENTLEMEN HEAH'S GONNA 'SPLAIN WHY THEY'S GOT THE LEGAL RIGHT TA...
AHEM. AH, YES MA'AM. YA SEE, WE DISCOVERED A LITTLE LOOPHOLE IN RELATION TO YOUR PARTICULAH AH... SITUATION.
NOW WE TRIED TO SETTLE THIS AMICABLY, WE ALL DID, BUT...

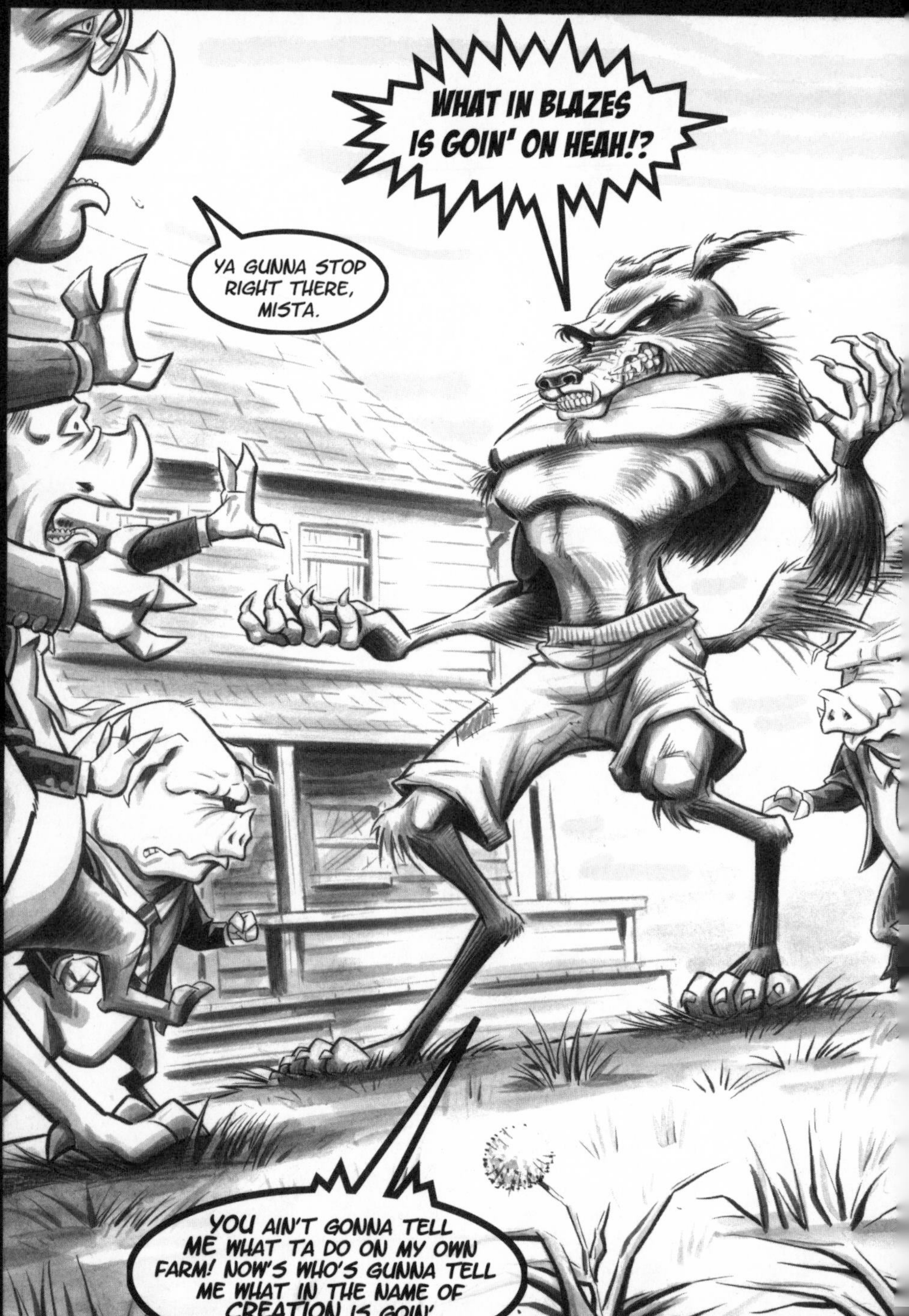
WHAT IN BLAZES IS GOIN' ON HEAH!?
YA GUNNA STOP RIGHT THERE, MISTA.
YOU AIN'T GONNA TELL ME WHAT TA DO ON MY OWN FARM! NOW'S WHO'S GUNNA TELL ME WHAT IN THE NAME OF CREATION IS GOIN' ON HEAH!?

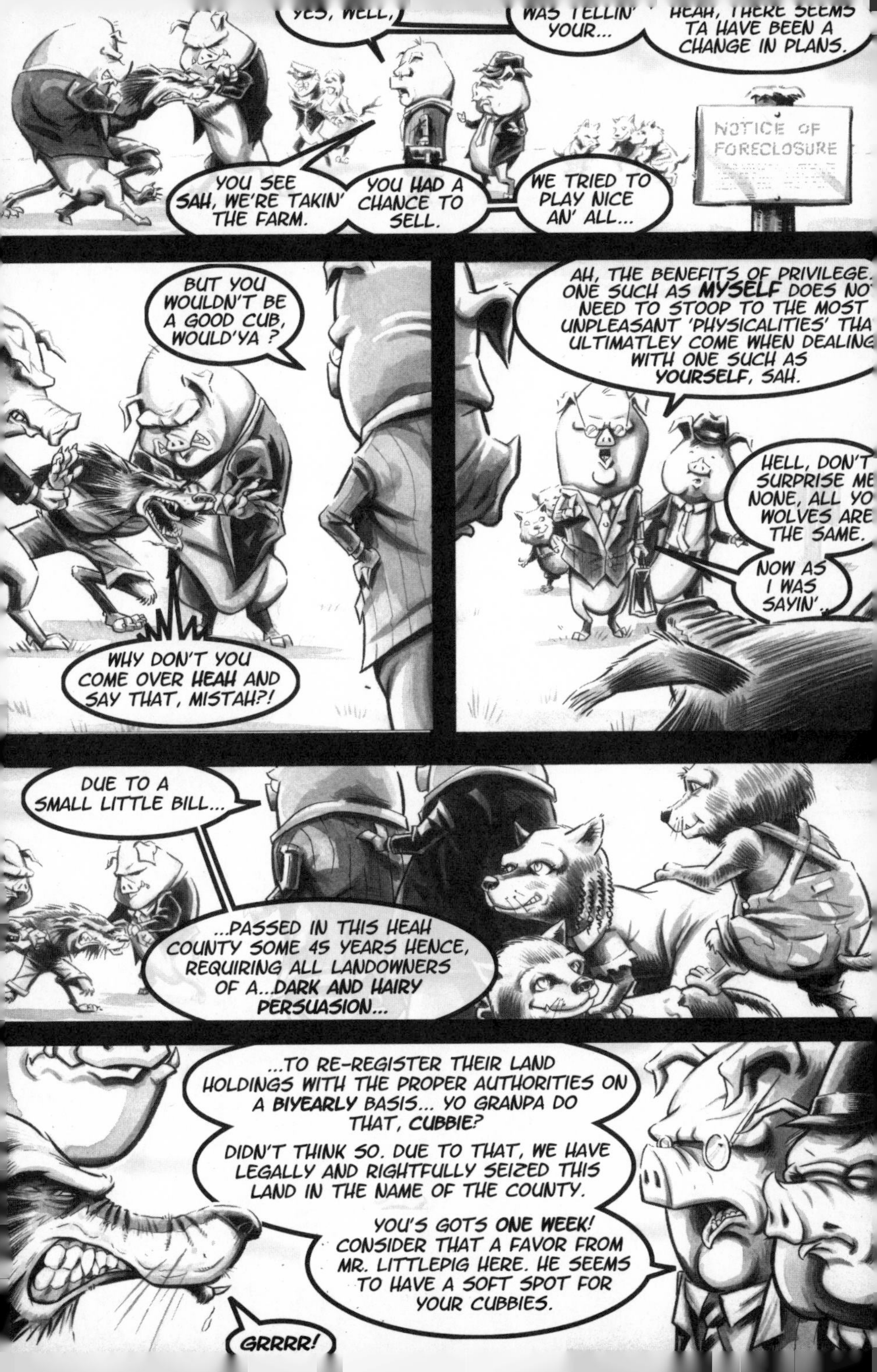
YES, WELL,
WAS TELLIN' YOUR...
HEAH, THERE SEEMS TA HAVE BEEN A CHANGE IN PLANS.
NOTICE OF FORECLOSURE
YOU SEE SAH, WE'RE TAKIN' THE FARM.
YOU HAD A CHANCE TO SELL.
WE TRIED TO PLAY NICE AN' ALL...
BUT YOU WOULDN'T BE A GOOD CUB, WOULD'YA ?
WHY DON'T YOU COME OVER HEAH AND SAY THAT, MISTAH?!
AH, THE BENEFITS OF PRIVILEGE. ONE SUCH AS MYSELF DOES NO NEED TO STOOP TO THE MOST UNPLEASANT 'PHYSICALITIES' THA ULTIMATLEY COME WHEN DEALING WITH ONE SUCH AS YOURSELF, SAH.
HELL, DON'T SURPRISE ME NONE, ALL YO WOLVES ARE THE SAME.
NOW AS I WAS SAYIN'...
DUE TO A SMALL LITTLE BILL...
...PASSED IN THIS HEAH COUNTY SOME 45 YEARS HENCE, REQUIRING ALL LANDOWNERS OF A...DARK AND HAIRY PERSUASION...
...TO RE-REGISTER THEIR LAND HOLDINGS WITH THE PROPER AUTHORITIES ON A BIYEARLY BASIS... YO GRANPA DO THAT, CUBBIE?
DIDN'T THINK SO. DUE TO THAT, WE HAVE LEGALLY AND RIGHTFULLY SEIZED THIS LAND IN THE NAME OF THE COUNTY.
YOU'S GOTS ONE WEEK! CONSIDER THAT A FAVOR FROM MR. LITTLEPIG HERE. HE SEEMS TO HAVE A SOFT SPOT FOR YOUR CUBBIES.
GRRRR!

HEY!
GIVE THAT BACK!
YOU CAN'T DO THIS!
THIS HEAH IS OUR FARM! OUR HOME!
WE OWN IT! YOU COME BACK HEAH AND I'LL...
NOW SEE HERE! THAT IS NOT A TOY! THAT...HEY STOP IT! THAT IS A VERY EXPENSIVE...
YOU'LL DO WHAT, CUB?
GRRRRR

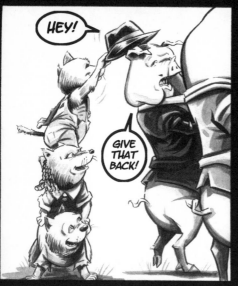

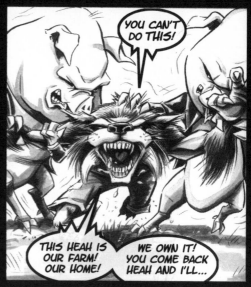

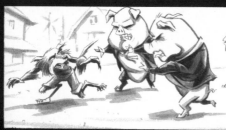

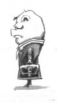

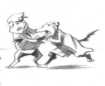

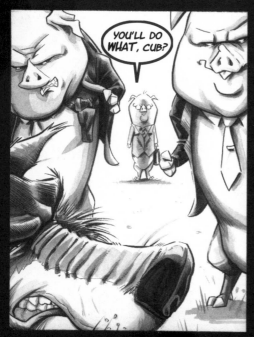

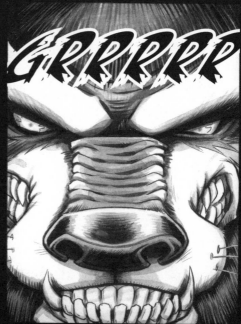

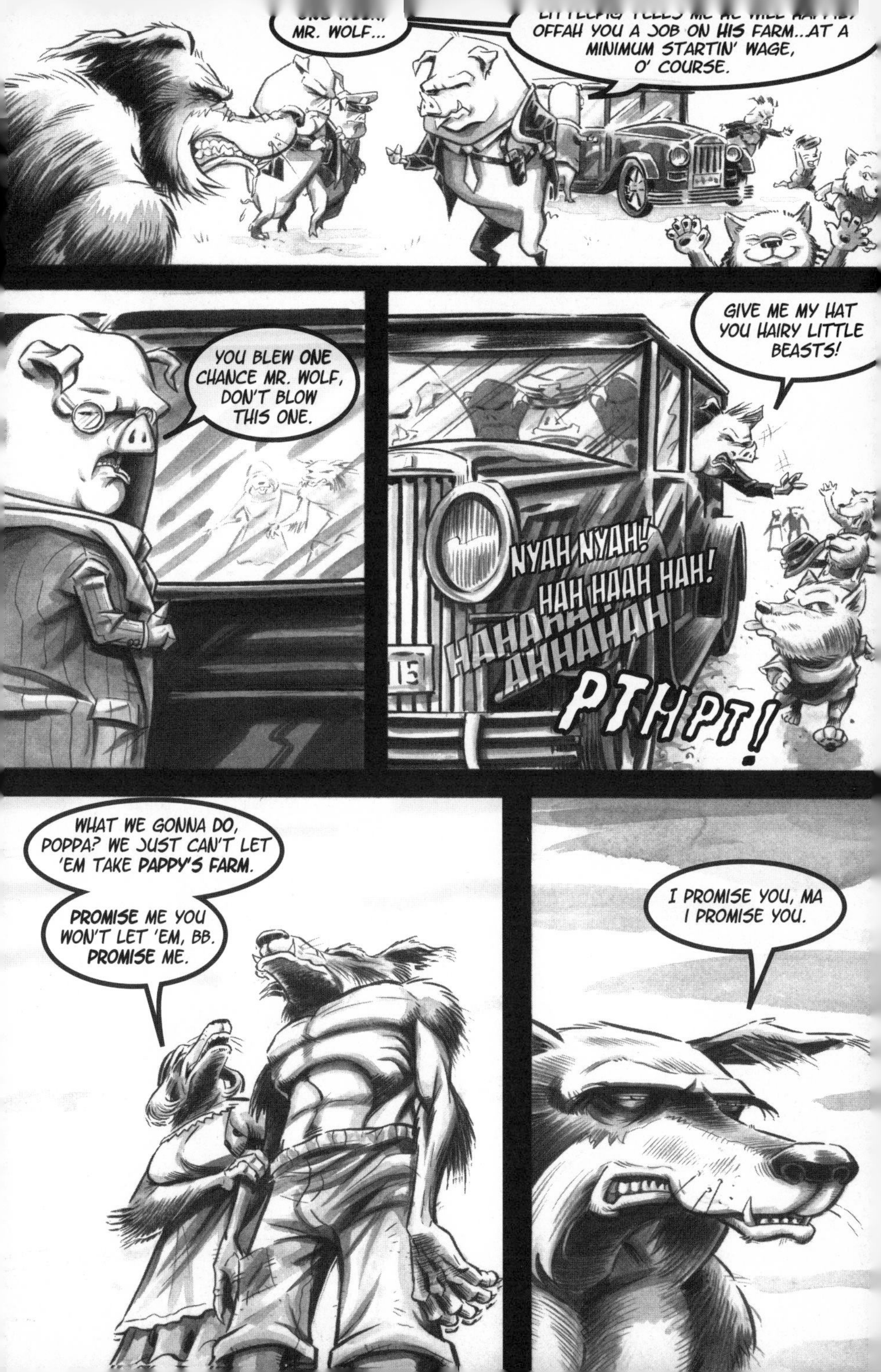

MR. WOLF...
OFFAH YOU A JOB ON HIS FARM..AT A MINIMUM STARTIN' WAGE, O' COURSE.
YOU BLEW ONE CHANCE MR. WOLF, DON'T BLOW THIS ONE.
GIVE ME MY HAT YOU HAIRY LITTLE BEASTS!
NYAH NYAH!
HAH HAAH HAH!
HAHAHAHAH AHHAHAH
PTHPT!
WHAT WE GONNA DO, POPPA? WE JUST CAN'T LET 'EM TAKE PAPPY'S FARM.
PROMISE ME YOU WON'T LET 'EM, BB. PROMISE ME.
I PROMISE YOU, MA I PROMISE YOU.

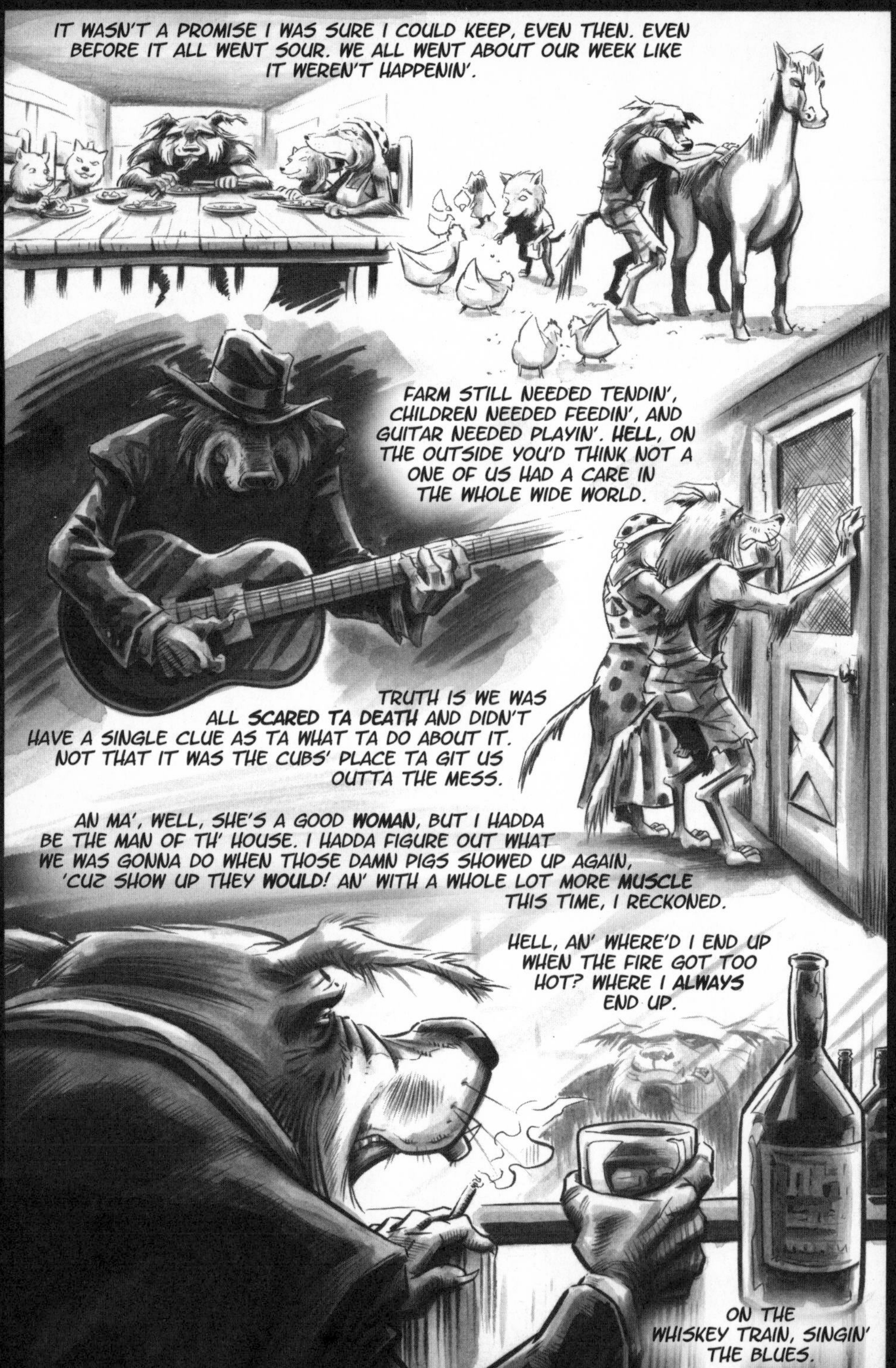
IT WASN'T A PROMISE I WAS SURE I COULD KEEP, EVEN THEN. EVEN BEFORE IT ALL WENT SOUR. WE ALL WENT ABOUT OUR WEEK LIKE IT WEREN'T HAPPENIN'.
FARM STILL NEEDED TENDIN', CHILDREN NEEDED FEEDIN', AND GUITAR NEEDED PLAYIN'. HELL, ON THE OUTSIDE YOU'D THINK NOT A ONE OF US HAD A CARE IN THE WHOLE WIDE WORLD.
TRUTH IS WE WAS ALL SCARED TA DEATH AND DIDN'T HAVE A SINGLE CLUE AS TA WHAT TA DO ABOUT IT. NOT THAT IT WAS THE CUBS' PLACE TA GIT US OUTTA THE MESS.
AN MA', WELL, SHE'S A GOOD WOMAN, BUT I HADDA BE THE MAN OF TH' HOUSE. I HADDA FIGURE OUT WHAT WE WAS GONNA DO WHEN THOSE DAMN PIGS SHOWED UP AGAIN, 'CUZ SHOW UP THEY WOULD! AN' WITH A WHOLE LOT MORE MUSCLE THIS TIME, I RECKONED.
HELL, AN' WHERE'D I END UP WHEN THE FIRE GOT TOO HOT? WHERE I ALWAYS END UP.
ON THE WHISKEY TRAIN, SINGIN' THE BLUES.

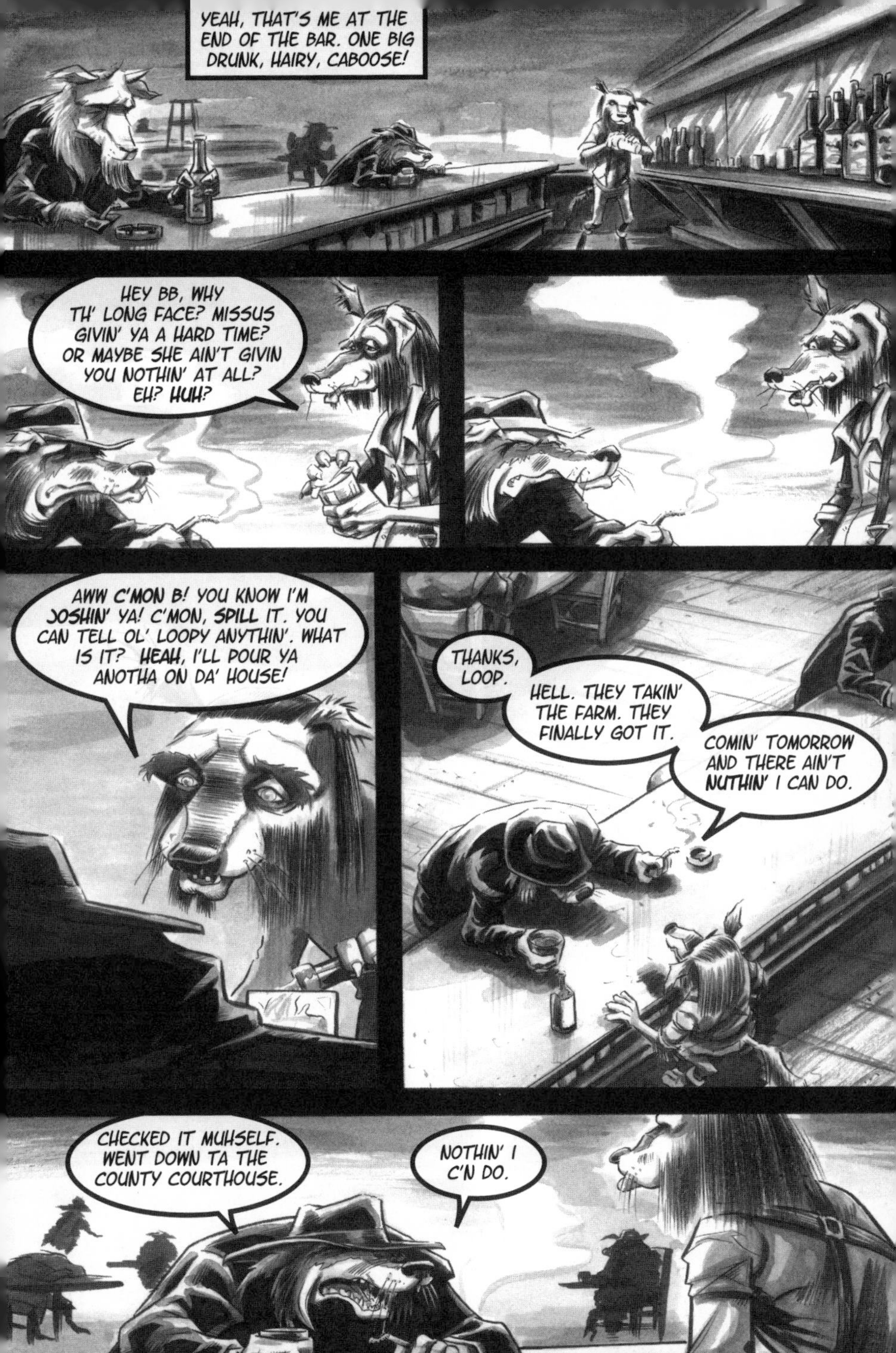
YEAH, THAT'S ME AT THE END OF THE BAR. ONE BIG DRUNK, HAIRY, CABOOSE!
HEY BB, WHY TH' LONG FACE? MISSUS GIVIN' YA A HARD TIME? OR MAYBE SHE AIN'T GIVIN YOU NOTHIN' AT ALL? EH? HUH?
AWW C'MON B! YOU KNOW I'M JOSHIN' YA! C'MON, SPILL IT. YOU CAN TELL OL' LOOPY ANYTHIN'. WHAT IS IT? HEAH, I'LL POUR YA ANOTHA ON DA' HOUSE!
THANKS, LOOP.
HELL. THEY TAKIN' THE FARM. THEY FINALLY GOT IT.
COMIN' TOMORROW AND THERE AIN'T NUTHIN' I CAN DO.
CHECKED IT MUHSELF. WENT DOWN TA THE COUNTY COURTHOUSE.
NOTHIN' I C'N DO.

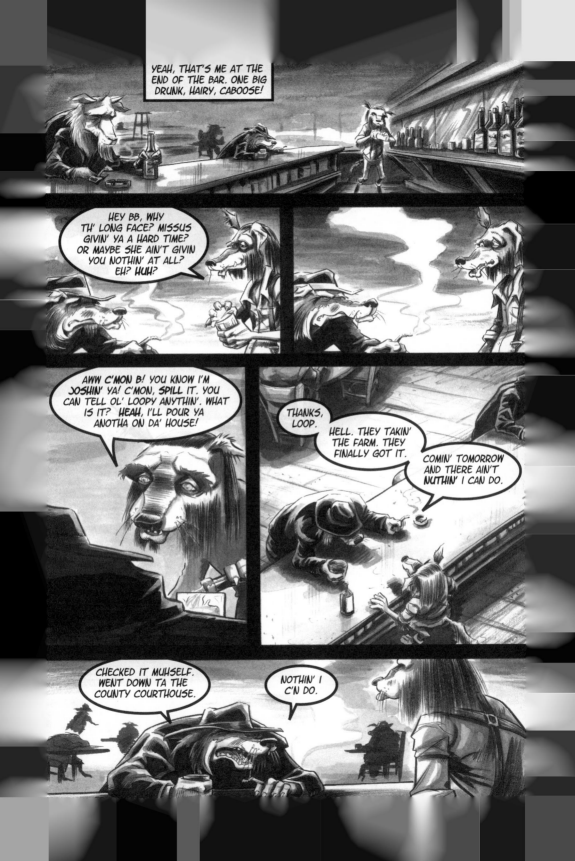

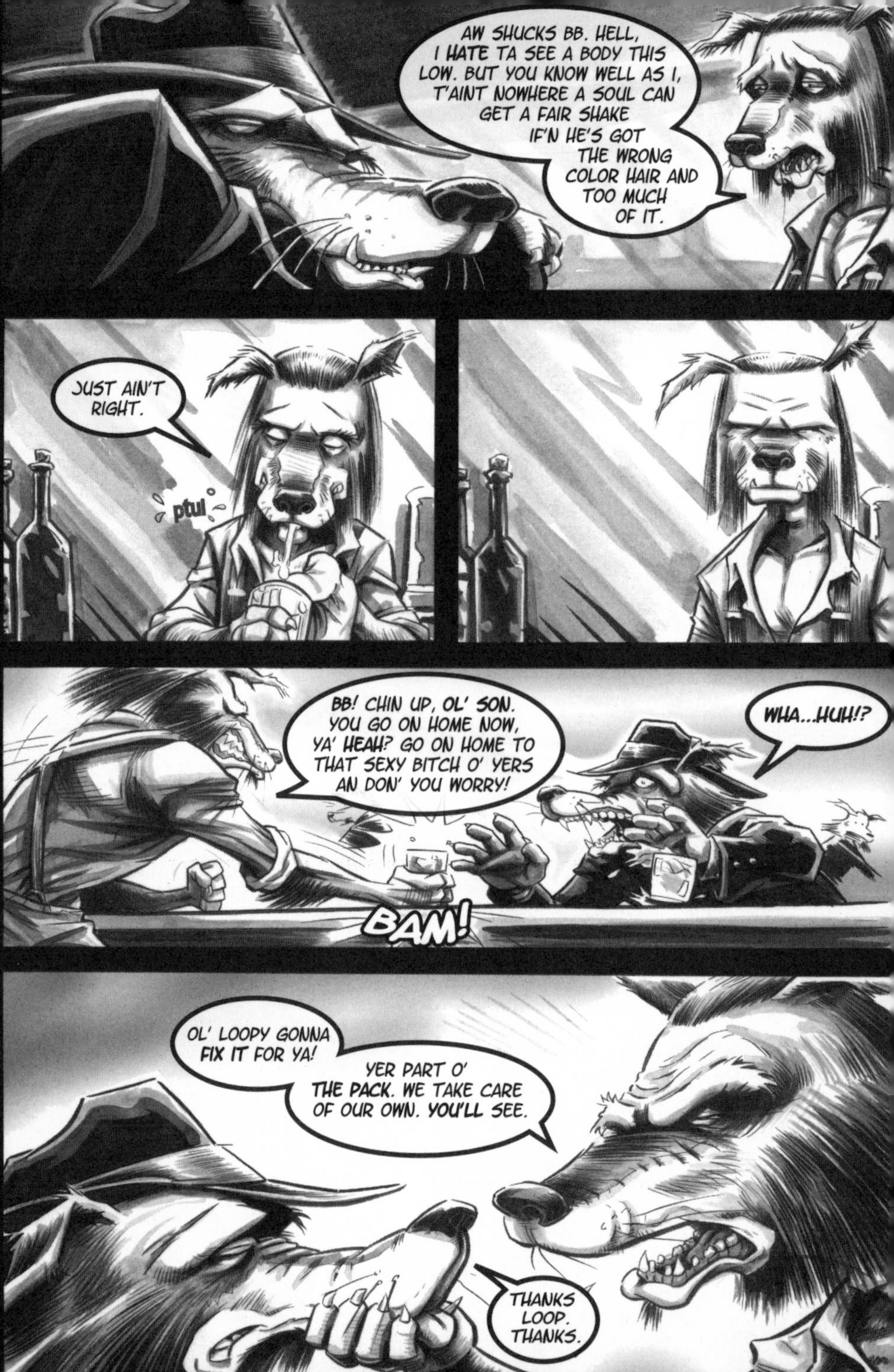
AW SHUCKS BB. HELL, I HATE TA SEE A BODY THIS LOW. BUT YOU KNOW WELL AS I, T'AINT NOWHERE A SOUL CAN GET A FAIR SHAKE IF'N HE'S GOT THE WRONG COLOR HAIR AND TOO MUCH OF IT.
JUST AIN'T RIGHT.
ptui
BB! CHIN UP, OL' SON. YOU GO ON HOME NOW, YA' HEAH? GO ON HOME TO THAT SEXY BITCH O' YERS AN DON' YOU WORRY!
WHA...HUH!?
BAM!
OL' LOOPY GONNA FIX IT FOR YA!
YER PART O' THE PACK. WE TAKE CARE OF OUR OWN. YOU'LL SEE.
THANKS LOOP. THANKS.

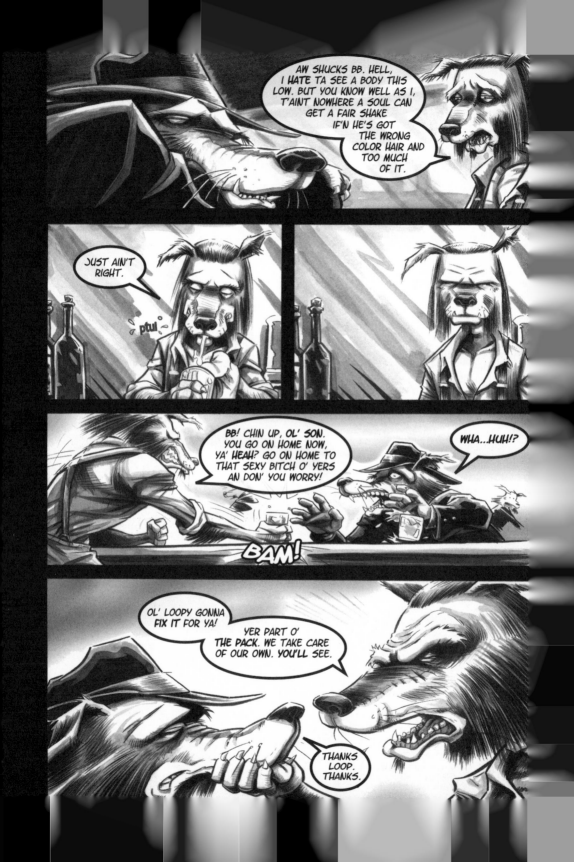

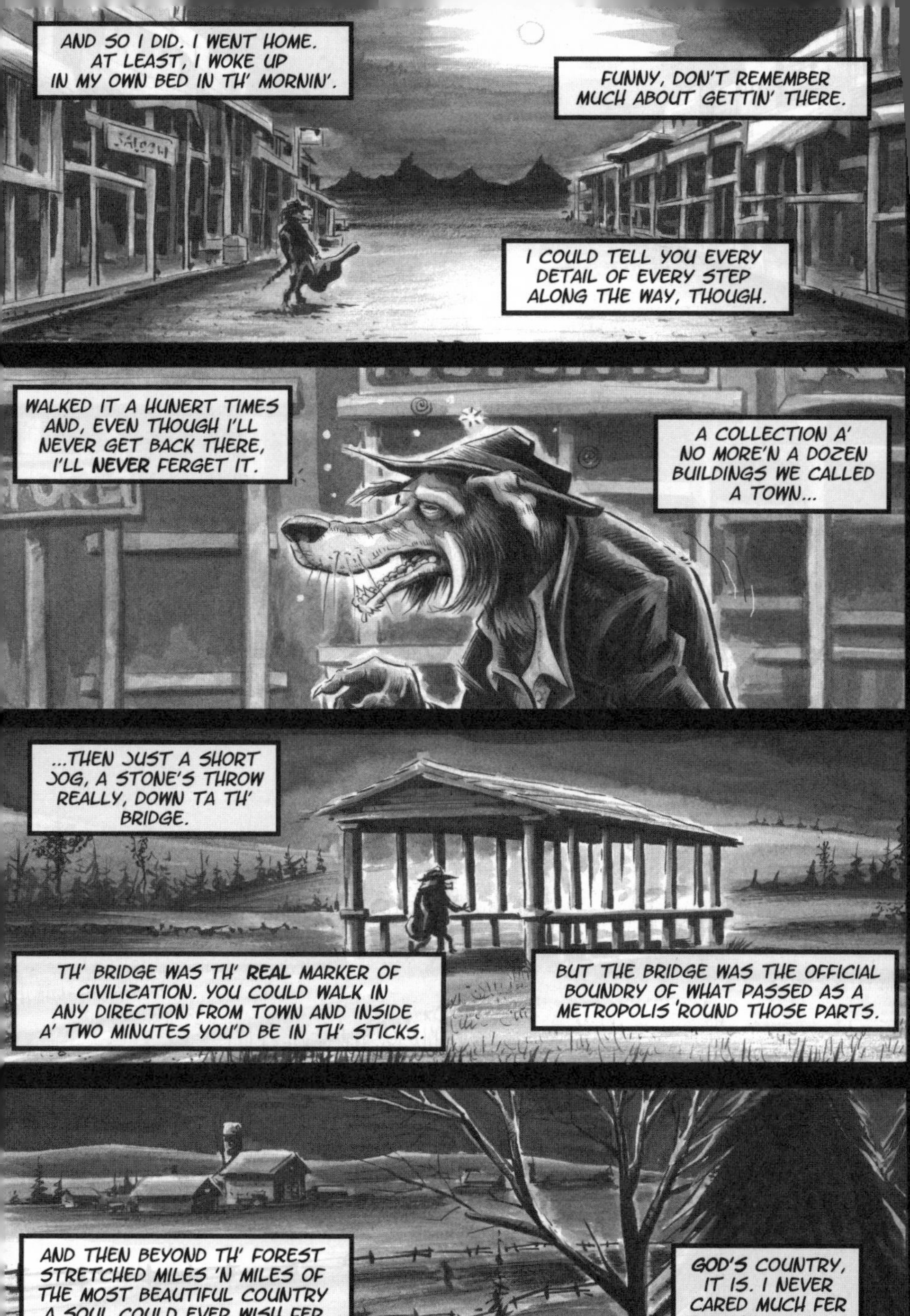
AND SO I DID. I WENT HOME. AT LEAST, I WOKE UP IN MY OWN BED IN TH' MORNIN'.
FUNNY, DON'T REMEMBER MUCH ABOUT GETTIN' THERE.
I COULD TELL YOU EVERY DETAIL OF EVERY STEP ALONG THE WAY, THOUGH.
WALKED IT A HUNERT TIMES AND, EVEN THOUGH I'LL NEVER GET BACK THERE, I'LL **NEVER** FERGET IT.
A COLLECTION A' NO MORE'N A DOZEN BUILDINGS WE CALLED A TOWN...
...THEN JUST A SHORT JOG, A STONE'S THROW REALLY, DOWN TA TH' BRIDGE.
TH' BRIDGE WAS TH' **REAL** MARKER OF CIVILIZATION. YOU COULD WALK IN ANY DIRECTION FROM TOWN AND INSIDE A' TWO MINUTES YOU'D BE IN TH' STICKS.
BUT THE BRIDGE WAS THE OFFICIAL BOUNDRY OF WHAT PASSED AS A METROPOLIS 'ROUND THOSE PARTS.
AND THEN BEYOND TH' FOREST STRETCHED MILES 'N MILES OF THE MOST BEAUTIFUL COUNTRY A SOUL COULD EVER WISH FER.
GOD'S COUNTRY, IT IS. I NEVER CARED MUCH FER FARMIN' YA KNOW, BUT I SURE DO MISS THE FARM.

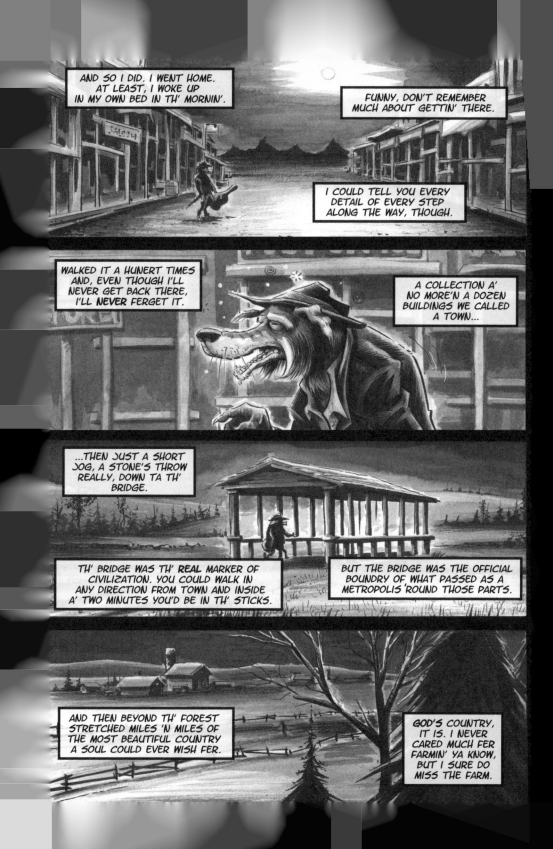

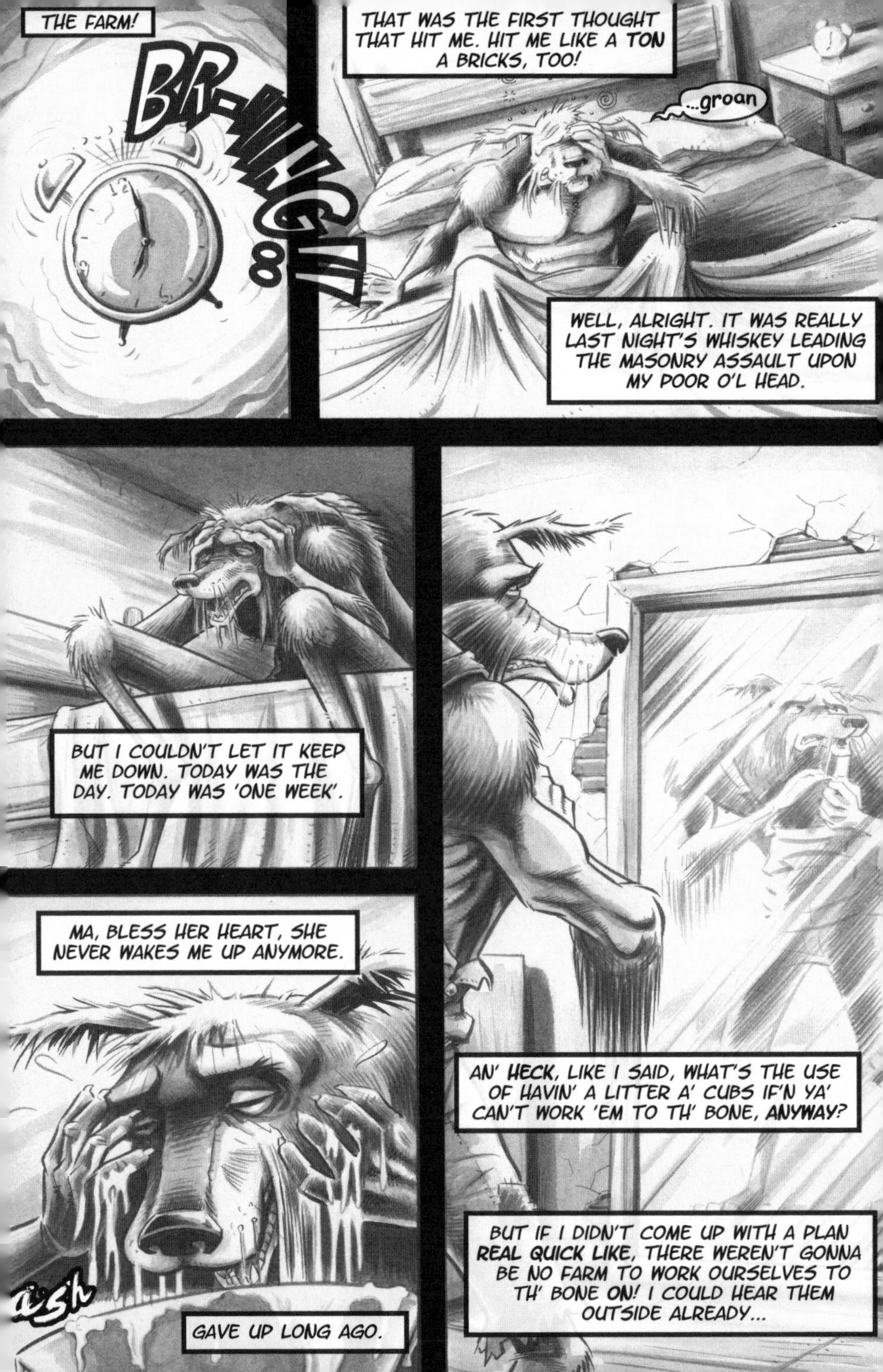
THE FARM!
BR-RINNG!!
THAT WAS THE FIRST THOUGHT THAT HIT ME. HIT ME LIKE A TON A BRICKS, TOO!
...groan
WELL, ALRIGHT. IT WAS REALLY LAST NIGHT'S WHISKEY LEADING THE MASONRY ASSAULT UPON MY POOR O'L HEAD.
BUT I COULDN'T LET IT KEEP ME DOWN. TODAY WAS THE DAY. TODAY WAS 'ONE WEEK'.
MA, BLESS HER HEART, SHE NEVER WAKES ME UP ANYMORE.
GAVE UP LONG AGO.
AN' HECK, LIKE I SAID, WHAT'S THE USE OF HAVIN' A LITTER A' CUBS IF'N YA' CAN'T WORK 'EM TO TH' BONE, ANYWAY?
BUT IF I DIDN'T COME UP WITH A PLAN REAL QUICK LIKE, THERE WEREN'T GONNA BE NO FARM TO WORK OURSELVES TO TH' BONE ON! I COULD HEAR THEM OUTSIDE ALREADY...

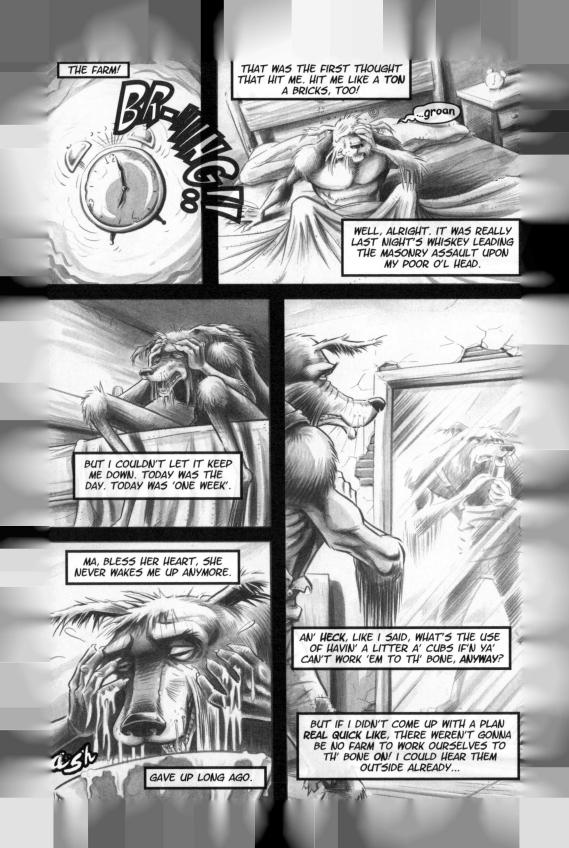

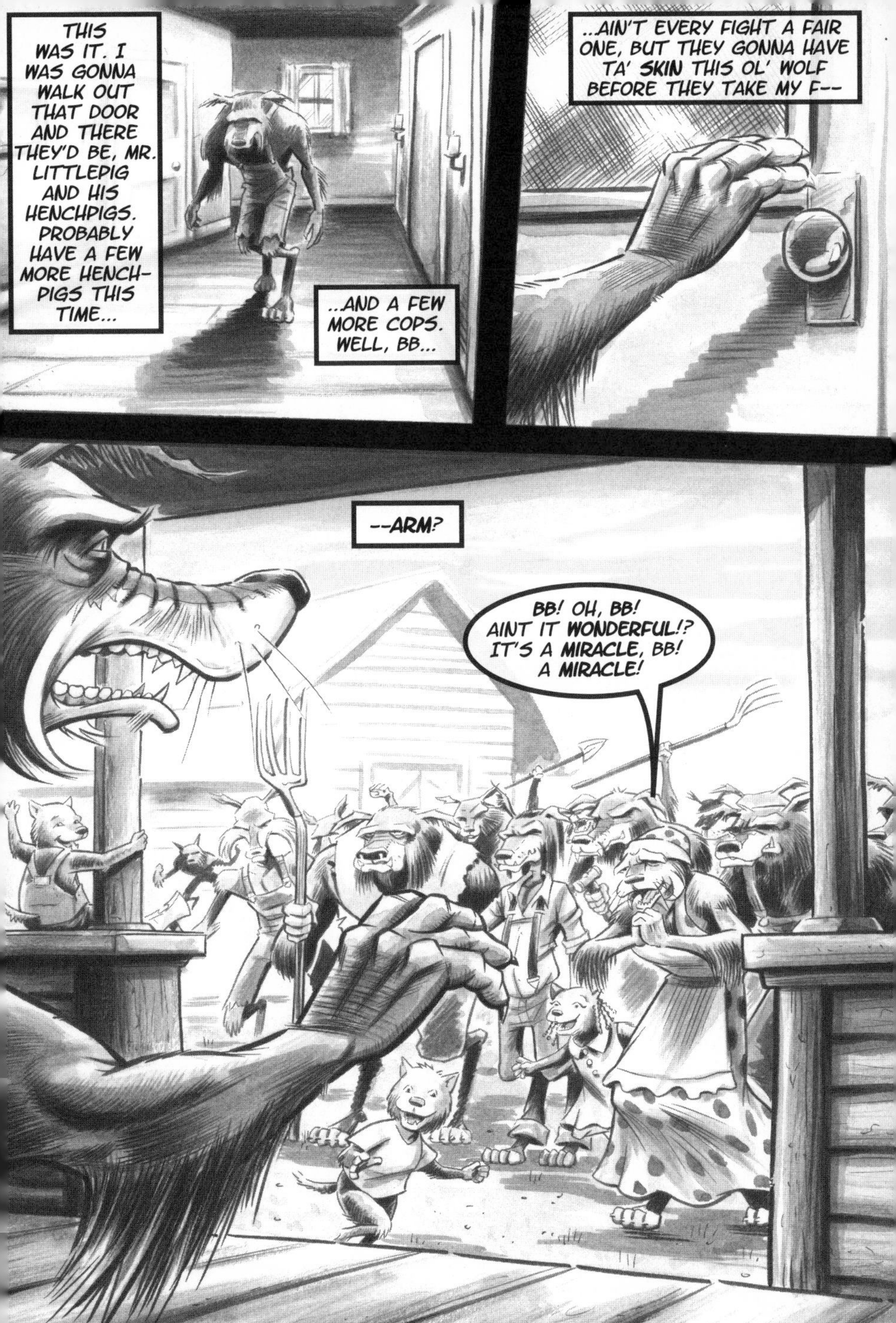
THIS WAS IT. I WAS GONNA WALK OUT THAT DOOR AND THERE THEY'D BE, MR. LITTLEPIG AND HIS HENCHPIGS. PROBABLY HAVE A FEW MORE HENCH-PIGS THIS TIME...
...AND A FEW MORE COPS. WELL, BB...
...AIN'T EVERY FIGHT A FAIR ONE, BUT THEY GONNA HAVE TA' SKIN THIS OL' WOLF BEFORE THEY TAKE MY F--
--ARM?
BB! OH, BB! AINT IT WONDERFUL!? IT'S A MIRACLE, BB! A MIRACLE!

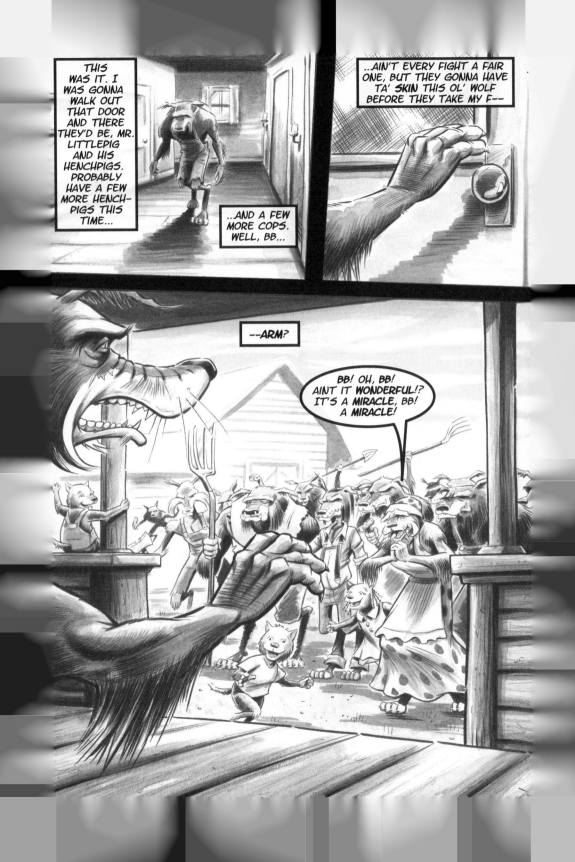

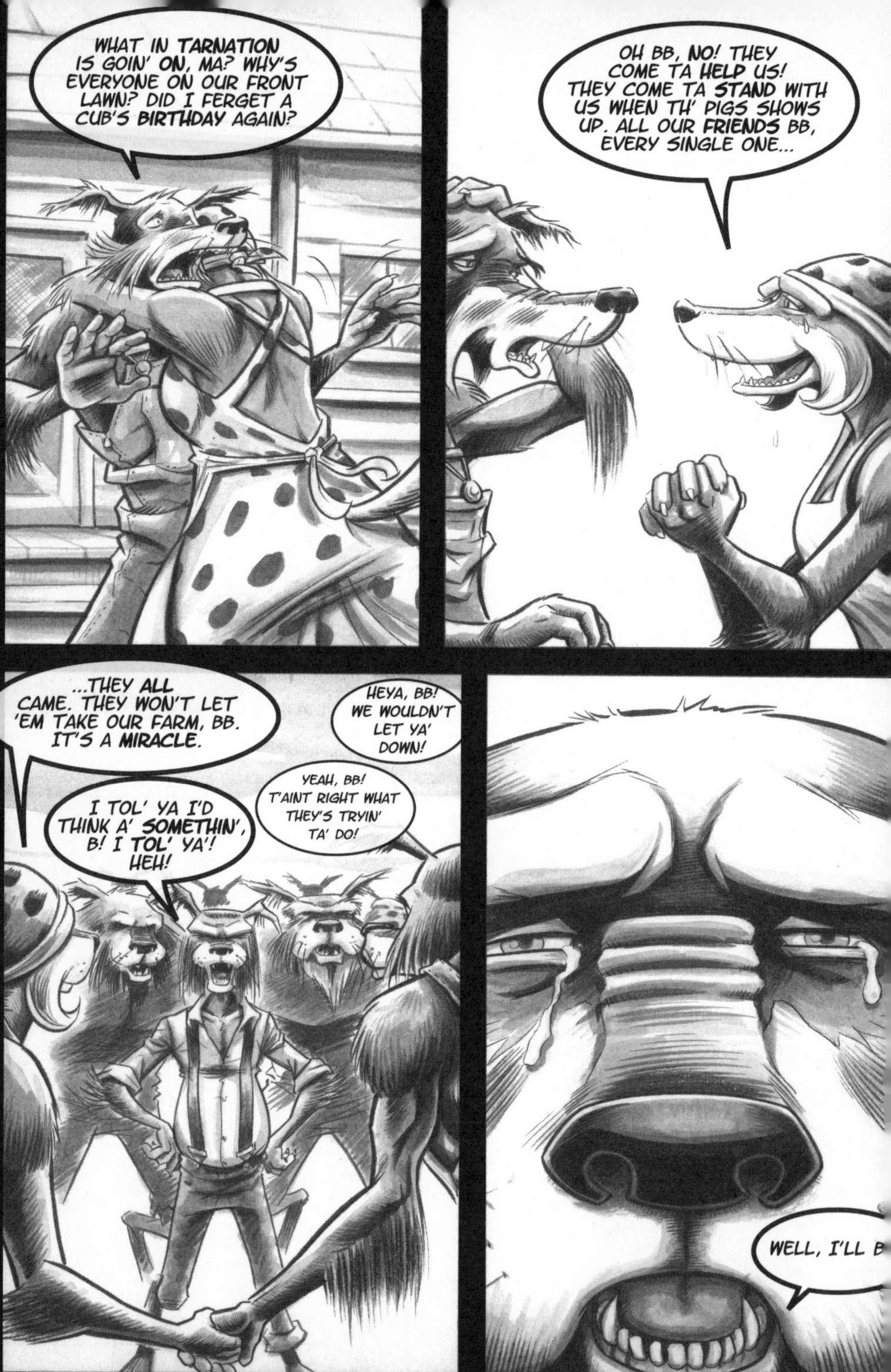
WHAT IN TARNATION IS GOIN' ON, MA? WHY'S EVERYONE ON OUR FRONT LAWN? DID I FERGET A CUB'S BIRTHDAY AGAIN?
OH BB, NO! THEY COME TA HELP US! THEY COME TA STAND WITH US WHEN TH' PIGS SHOWS UP. ALL OUR FRIENDS BB, EVERY SINGLE ONE...
...THEY ALL CAME. THEY WON'T LET 'EM TAKE OUR FARM, BB. IT'S A MIRACLE.
HEYA, BB! WE WOULDN'T LET YA' DOWN!
YEAH, BB! T'AINT RIGHT WHAT THEY'S TRYIN' TA' DO!
I TOL' YA I'D THINK A' SOMETHIN', B! I TOL' YA'! HEH!
WELL, I'LL B

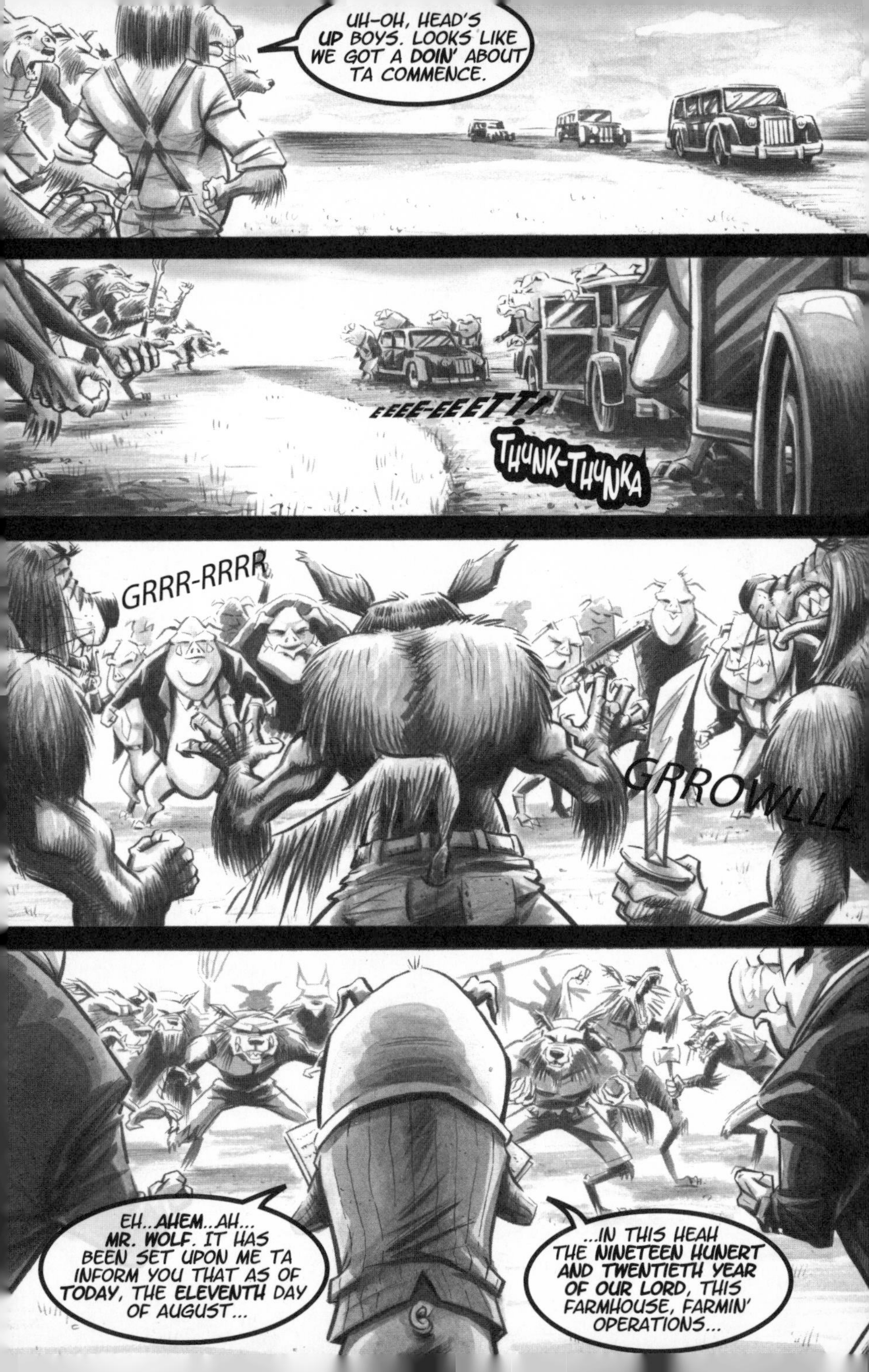
UH-OH, HEAD'S UP BOYS. LOOKS LIKE WE GOT A DOIN' ABOUT TA COMMENCE.
EEEE-EEETT!
THUNK-THUNKA
GRRR-RRRR
GRRROWLLL
EH..AHEM..AH... MR. WOLF. IT HAS BEEN SET UPON ME TA INFORM YOU THAT AS OF TODAY, THE ELEVENTH DAY OF AUGUST...
...IN THIS HEAH THE NINETEEN HUNERT AND TWENTIETH YEAR OF OUR LORD, THIS FARMHOUSE, FARMIN' OPERATIONS...

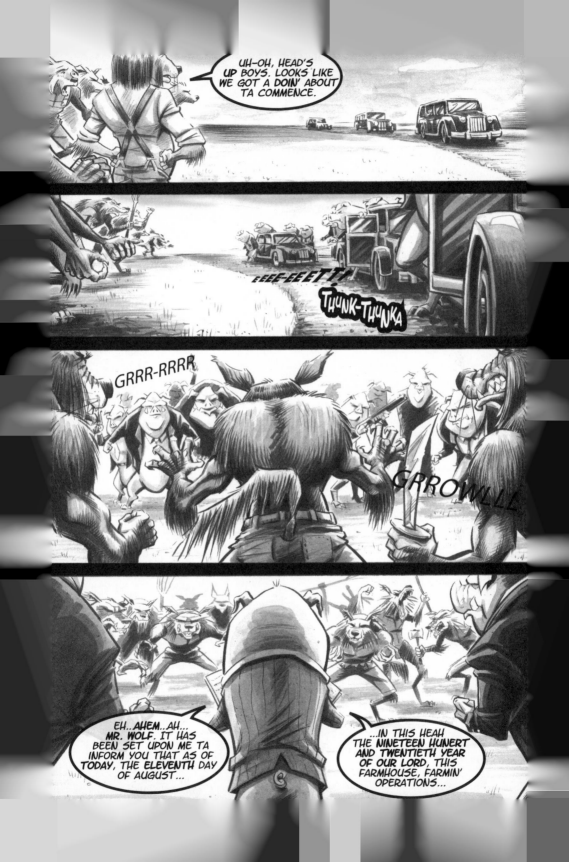

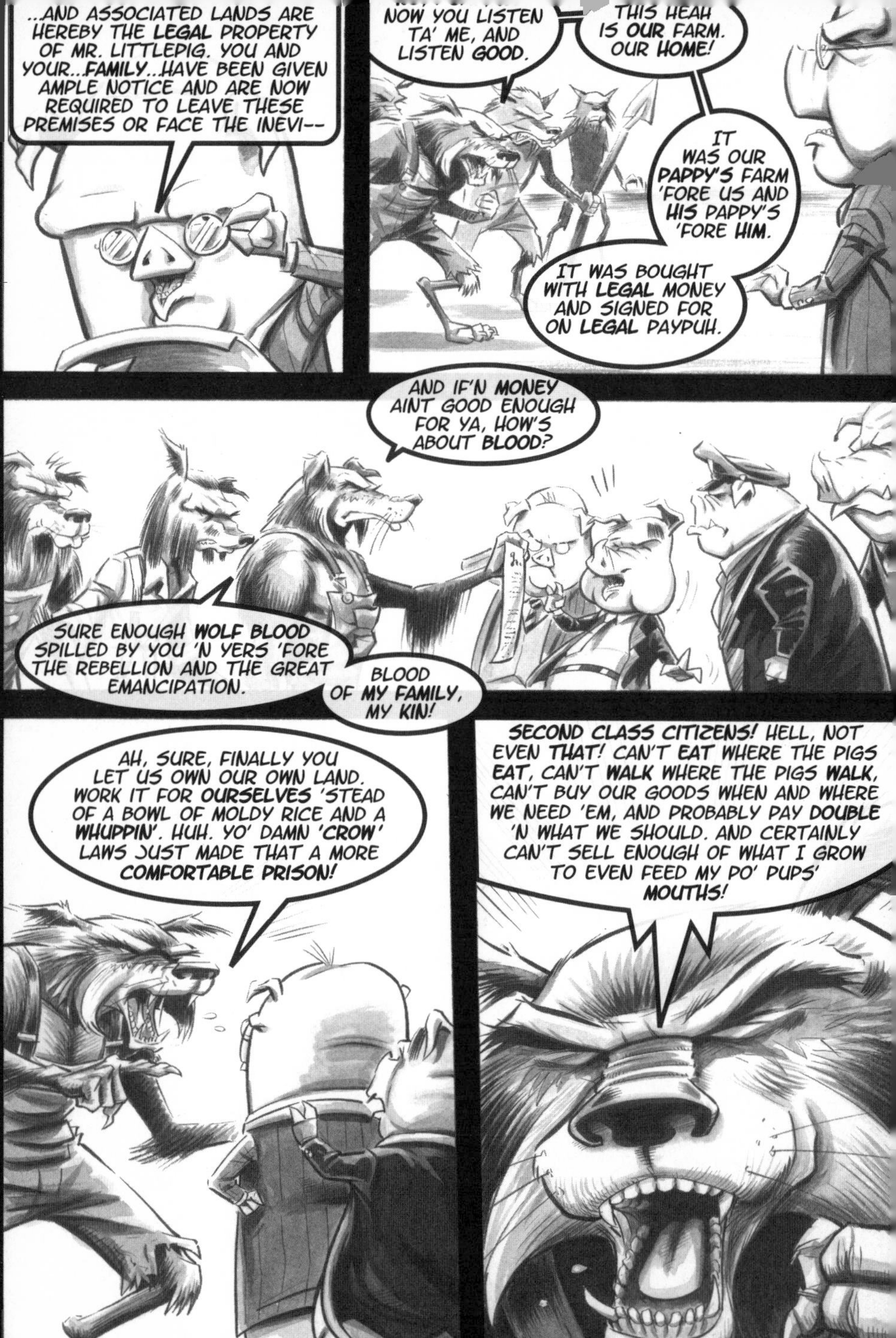
...AND ASSOCIATED LANDS ARE HEREBY THE LEGAL PROPERTY OF MR. LITTLEPIG. YOU AND YOUR...FAMILY...HAVE BEEN GIVEN AMPLE NOTICE AND ARE NOW REQUIRED TO LEAVE THESE PREMISES OR FACE THE INEVI--
NOW YOU LISTEN TA' ME, AND LISTEN GOOD.
THIS HEAH IS OUR FARM. OUR HOME!
IT WAS OUR PAPPY'S FARM 'FORE US AND HIS PAPPY'S 'FORE HIM.
IT WAS BOUGHT WITH LEGAL MONEY AND SIGNED FOR ON LEGAL PAYPUH.
AND IF'N MONEY AINT GOOD ENOUGH FOR YA, HOW'S ABOUT BLOOD?
SURE ENOUGH WOLF BLOOD SPILLED BY YOU 'N YERS 'FORE THE REBELLION AND THE GREAT EMANCIPATION.
BLOOD OF MY FAMILY, MY KIN!
AH, SURE, FINALLY YOU LET US OWN OUR OWN LAND. WORK IT FOR OURSELVES 'STEAD OF A BOWL OF MOLDY RICE AND A WHUPPIN'. HUH. YO' DAMN 'CROW' LAWS JUST MADE THAT A MORE COMFORTABLE PRISON!
SECOND CLASS CITIZENS! HELL, NOT EVEN THAT! CAN'T EAT WHERE THE PIGS EAT, CAN'T WALK WHERE THE PIGS WALK, CAN'T BUY OUR GOODS WHEN AND WHERE WE NEED 'EM, AND PROBABLY PAY DOUBLE 'N WHAT WE SHOULD. AND CERTAINLY CAN'T SELL ENOUGH OF WHAT I GROW TO EVEN FEED MY PO' PUPS' MOUTHS!

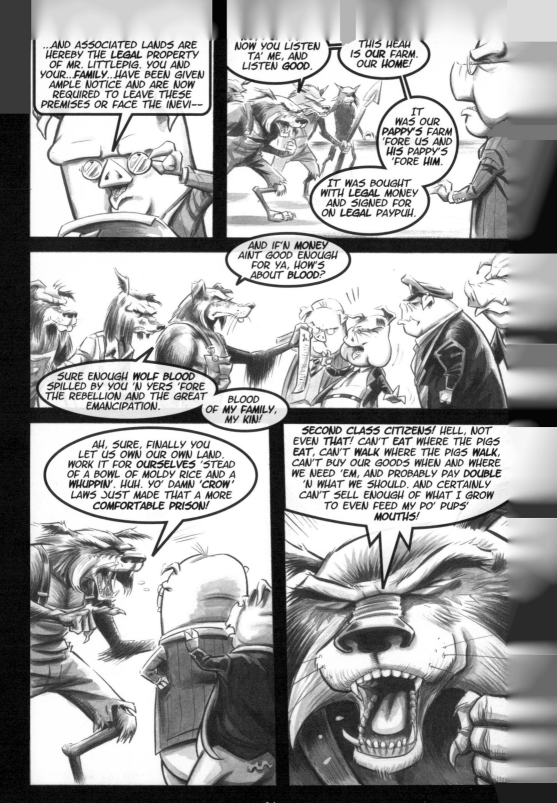

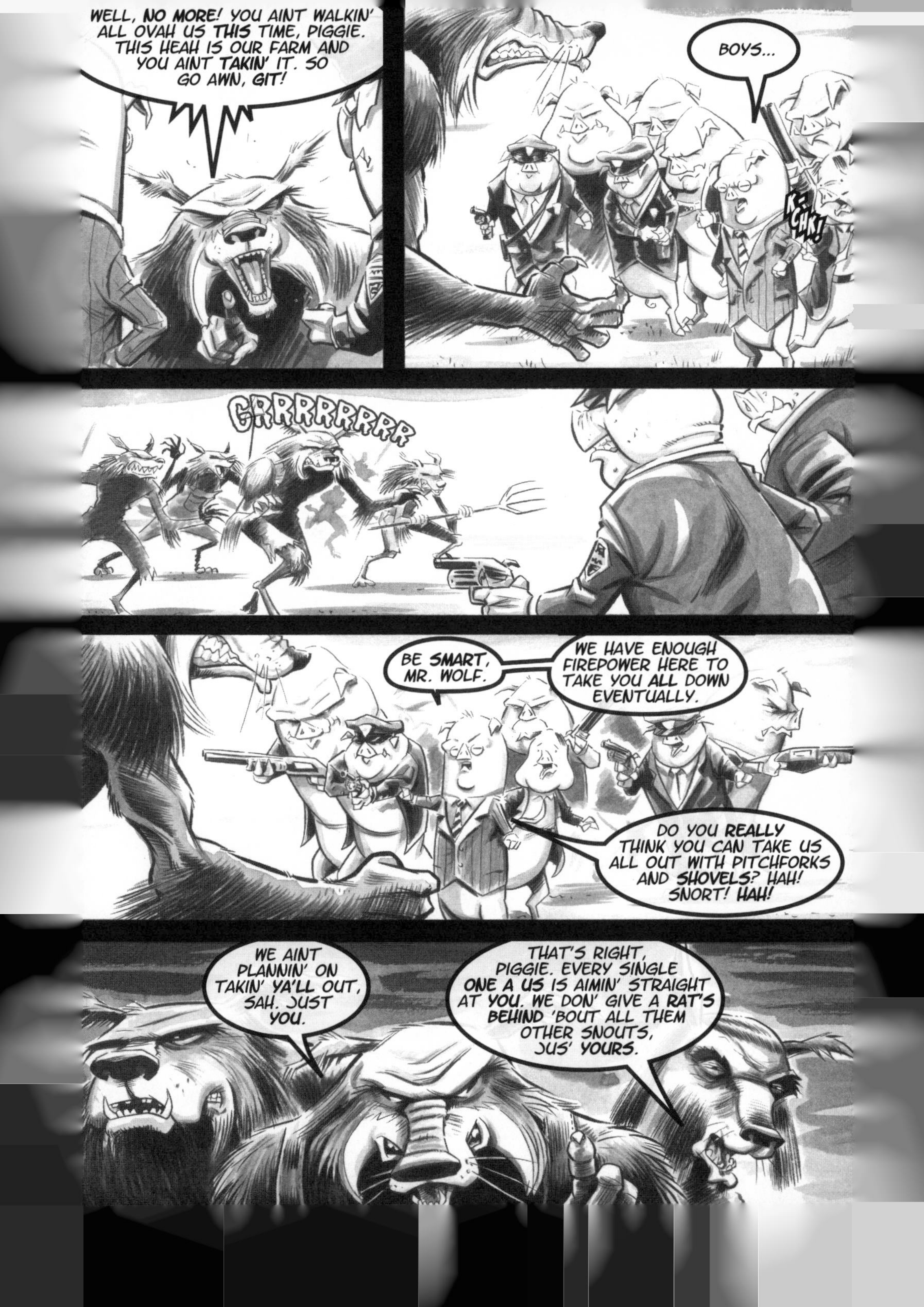

WELL, NO MORE! YOU AINT WALKIN' ALL OVAH US THIS TIME, PIGGIE. THIS HEAH IS OUR FARM AND YOU AINT TAKIN' IT. SO GO AWN, GIT!
BOYS...
K-CHK!
GRRRRRRRRR
BE SMART, MR. WOLF.
WE HAVE ENOUGH FIREPOWER HERE TO TAKE YOU ALL DOWN EVENTUALLY.
DO YOU REALLY THINK YOU CAN TAKE US ALL OUT WITH PITCHFORKS AND SHOVELS? HAH! SNORT! HAH!
WE AINT PLANNIN' ON TAKIN' YA'LL OUT, SAH. JUST YOU.
THAT'S RIGHT, PIGGIE. EVERY SINGLE ONE A US IS AIMIN' STRAIGHT AT YOU. WE DON' GIVE A RAT'S BEHIND 'BOUT ALL THEM OTHER SNOUTS, JUS' YOURS.

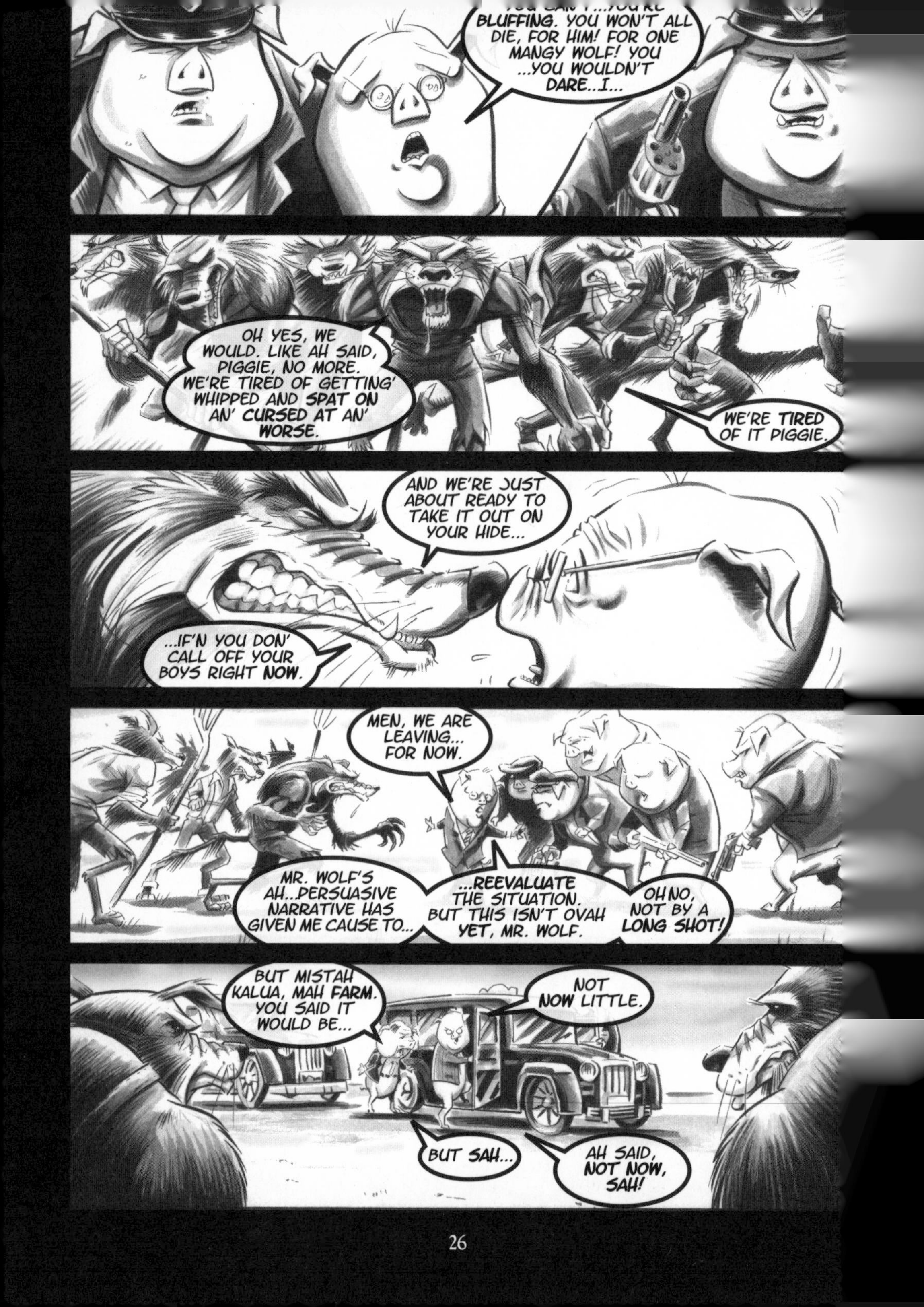
BLUFFING. YOU WON'T ALL DIE, FOR HIM! FOR ONE MANGY WOLF! YOU ...YOU WOULDN'T DARE...I...
OH YES, WE WOULD. LIKE AH SAID, PIGGIE, NO MORE. WE'RE TIRED OF GETTING' WHIPPED AND SPAT ON AN' CURSED AT AN' WORSE.
WE'RE TIRED OF IT PIGGIE.
AND WE'RE JUST ABOUT READY TO TAKE IT OUT ON YOUR HIDE...
...IF'N YOU DON' CALL OFF YOUR BOYS RIGHT NOW.
MEN, WE ARE LEAVING... FOR NOW.
MR. WOLF'S AH...PERSUASIVE NARRATIVE HAS GIVEN ME CAUSE TO...
...REEVALUATE THE SITUATION. BUT THIS ISN'T OVAH YET, MR. WOLF.
OH NO, NOT BY A LONG SHOT!
BUT MISTAH KALUA, MAH FARM. YOU SAID IT WOULD BE...
NOT NOW LITTLE.
BUT SAH...
AH SAID, NOT NOW, SAH!

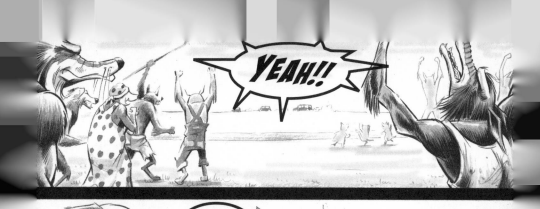

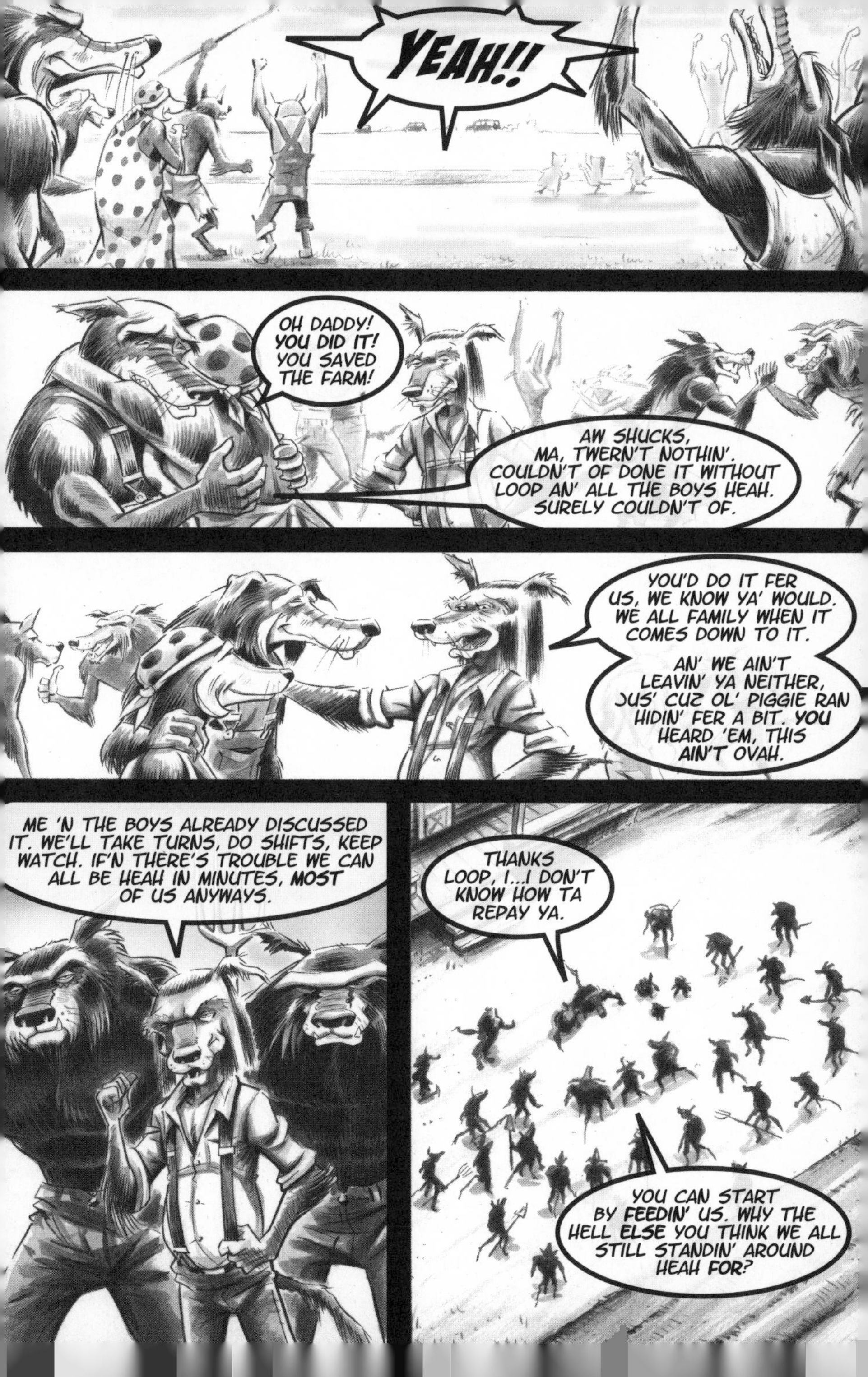
YEAH!!
OH DADDY! YOU DID IT! YOU SAVED THE FARM!
AW SHUCKS, MA, TWERN'T NOTHIN'. COULDN'T OF DONE IT WITHOUT LOOP AN' ALL THE BOYS HEAH. SURELY COULDN'T OF.
YOU'D DO IT FER US, WE KNOW YA' WOULD. WE ALL FAMILY WHEN IT COMES DOWN TO IT.
AN' WE AIN'T LEAVIN' YA NEITHER, JUS' CUZ OL' PIGGIE RAN HIDIN' FER A BIT. YOU HEARD 'EM, THIS AIN'T OVAH.
ME 'N THE BOYS ALREADY DISCUSSED IT. WE'LL TAKE TURNS, DO SHIFTS, KEEP WATCH. IF'N THERE'S TROUBLE WE CAN ALL BE HEAH IN MINUTES, MOST OF US ANYWAYS.
THANKS LOOP, I...I DON'T KNOW HOW TA REPAY YA.
YOU CAN START BY FEEDIN' US. WHY THE HELL ELSE YOU THINK WE ALL STILL STANDIN' AROUND HEAH FOR?

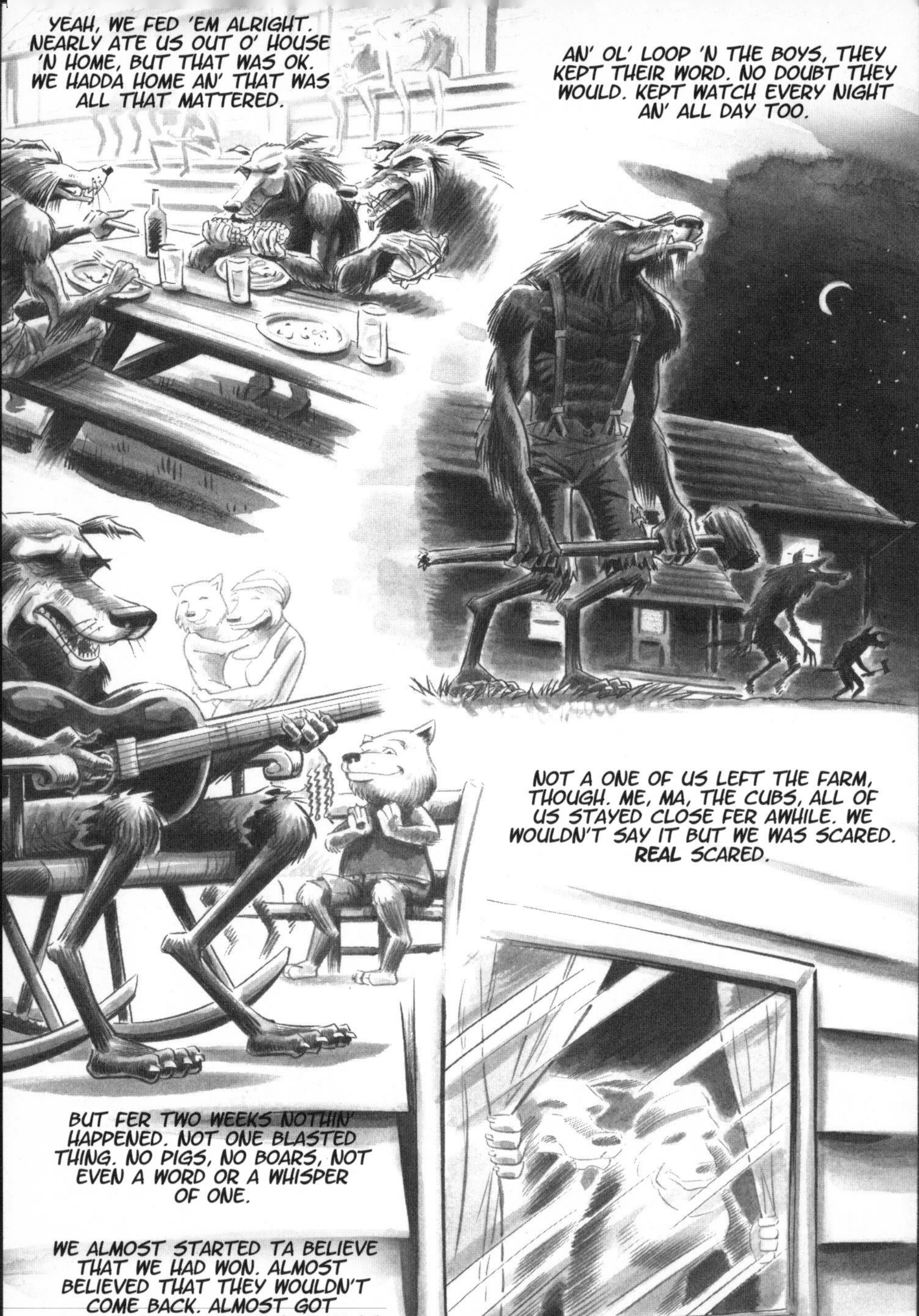
YEAH, WE FED 'EM ALRIGHT. NEARLY ATE US OUT O' HOUSE 'N HOME, BUT THAT WAS OK. WE HADDA HOME AN' THAT WAS ALL THAT MATTERED.
AN' OL' LOOP 'N THE BOYS, THEY KEPT THEIR WORD. NO DOUBT THEY WOULD. KEPT WATCH EVERY NIGHT AN' ALL DAY TOO.
NOT A ONE OF US LEFT THE FARM, THOUGH. ME, MA, THE CUBS, ALL OF US STAYED CLOSE FER AWHILE. WE WOULDN'T SAY IT BUT WE WAS SCARED. REAL SCARED.
BUT FER TWO WEEKS NOTHIN' HAPPENED. NOT ONE BLASTED THING. NO PIGS, NO BOARS, NOT EVEN A WORD OR A WHISPER OF ONE.
WE ALMOST STARTED TA BELIEVE THAT WE HAD WON. ALMOST BELIEVED THAT THEY WOULDN'T COME BACK. ALMOST GOT COMFORTABLE. I RECKON ALMOST IS ALL IT TAKES.

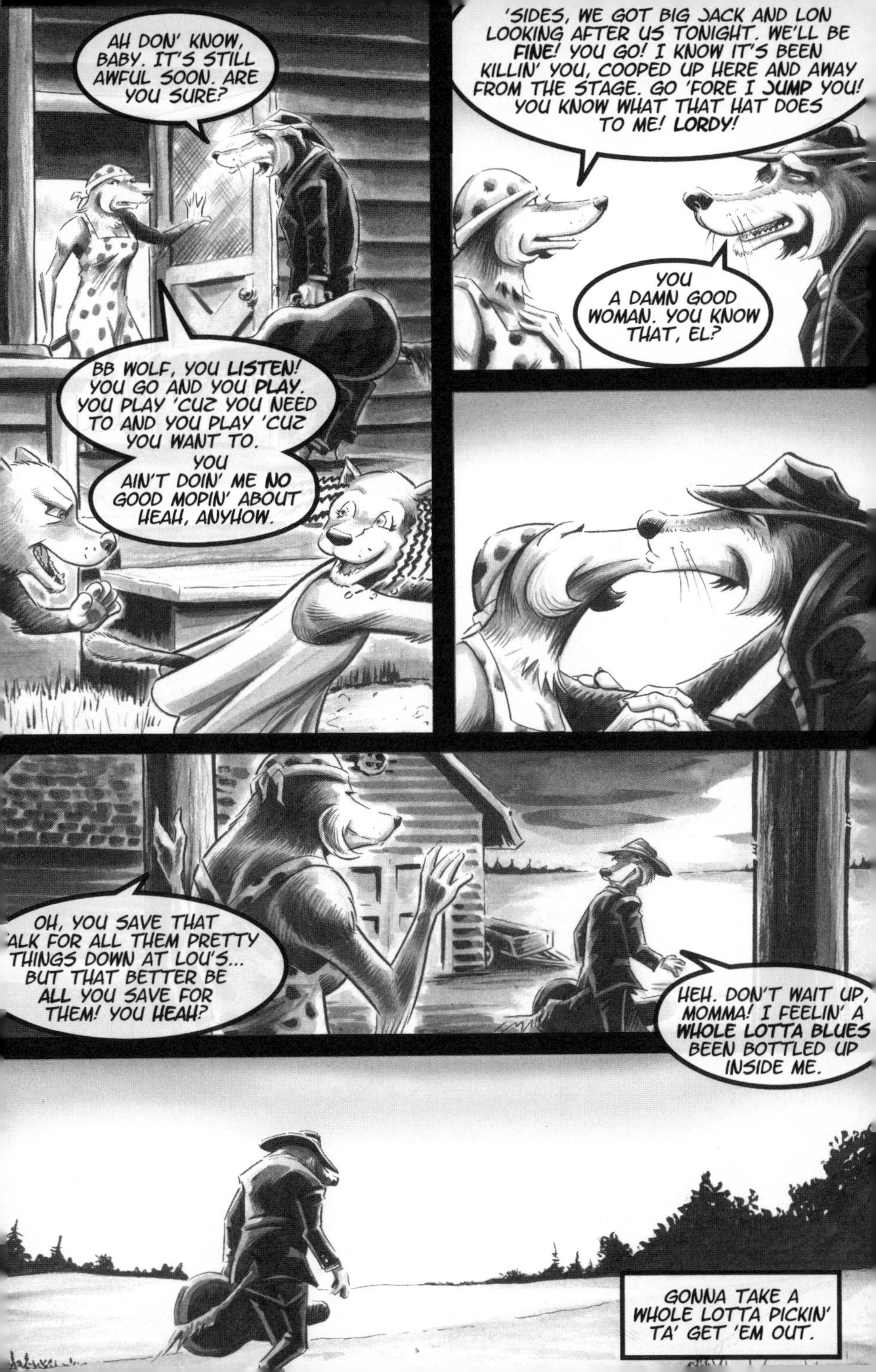
AH DON' KNOW, BABY. IT'S STILL AWFUL SOON. ARE YOU SURE?
BB WOLF, YOU LISTEN! YOU GO AND YOU PLAY. YOU PLAY 'CUZ YOU NEED TO AND YOU PLAY 'CUZ YOU WANT TO.
YOU AIN'T DOIN' ME NO GOOD MOPIN' ABOUT HEAH, ANYHOW.
'SIDES, WE GOT BIG JACK AND LON LOOKING AFTER US TONIGHT. WE'LL BE FINE! YOU GO! I KNOW IT'S BEEN KILLIN' YOU, COOPED UP HERE AND AWAY FROM THE STAGE. GO 'FORE I JUMP YOU! YOU KNOW WHAT THAT HAT DOES TO ME! LORDY!
YOU A DAMN GOOD WOMAN. YOU KNOW THAT, EL?
OH, YOU SAVE THAT TALK FOR ALL THEM PRETTY THINGS DOWN AT LOU'S... BUT THAT BETTER BE ALL YOU SAVE FOR THEM! YOU HEAH?
HEH. DON'T WAIT UP, MOMMA! I FEELIN' A WHOLE LOTTA BLUES BEEN BOTTLED UP INSIDE ME.
GONNA TAKE A WHOLE LOTTA PICKIN' TA' GET 'EM OUT.

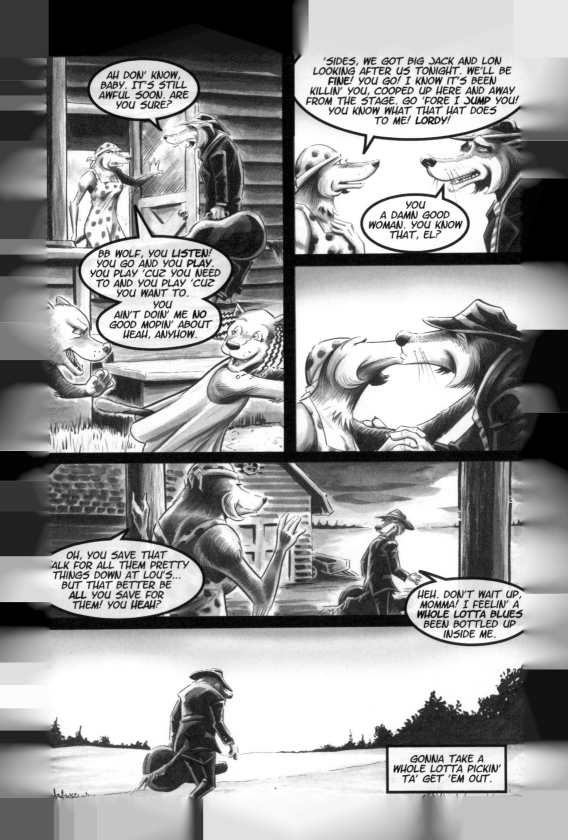

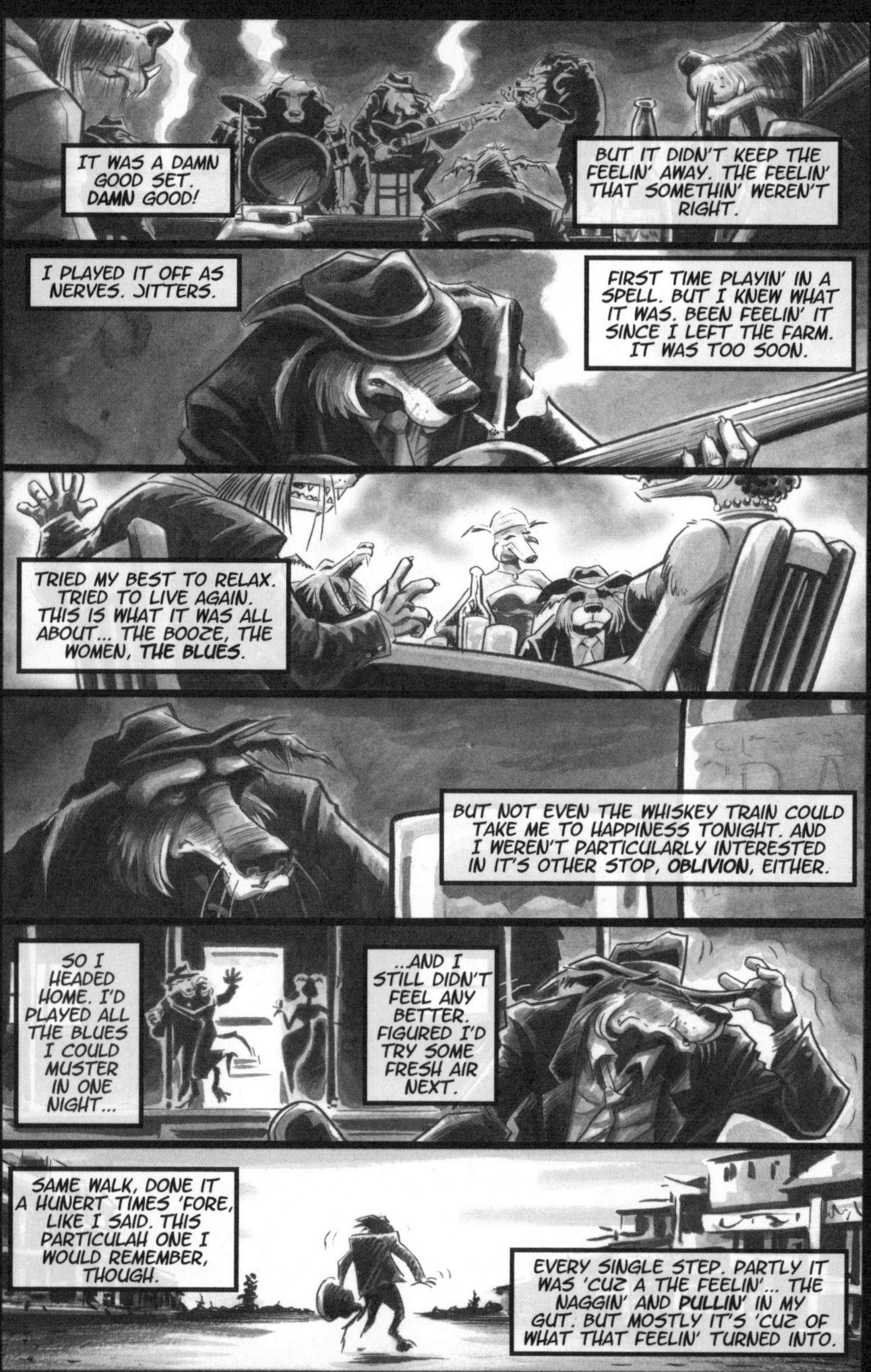
IT WAS A DAMN GOOD SET. DAMN GOOD!
BUT IT DIDN'T KEEP THE FEELIN' AWAY. THE FEELIN' THAT SOMETHIN' WEREN'T RIGHT.
I PLAYED IT OFF AS NERVES. JITTERS.
FIRST TIME PLAYIN' IN A SPELL. BUT I KNEW WHAT IT WAS. BEEN FEELIN' IT SINCE I LEFT THE FARM. IT WAS TOO SOON.
TRIED MY BEST TO RELAX. TRIED TO LIVE AGAIN. THIS IS WHAT IT WAS ALL ABOUT... THE BOOZE, THE WOMEN, THE BLUES.
BUT NOT EVEN THE WHISKEY TRAIN COULD TAKE ME TO HAPPINESS TONIGHT. AND I WEREN'T PARTICULARLY INTERESTED IN IT'S OTHER STOP, OBLIVION, EITHER.
SO I HEADED HOME. I'D PLAYED ALL THE BLUES I COULD MUSTER IN ONE NIGHT...
...AND I STILL DIDN'T FEEL ANY BETTER. FIGURED I'D TRY SOME FRESH AIR NEXT.
SAME WALK, DONE IT A HUNERT TIMES 'FORE, LIKE I SAID. THIS PARTICULAH ONE I WOULD REMEMBER, THOUGH.
EVERY SINGLE STEP. PARTLY IT WAS 'CUZ A THE FEELIN'... THE NAGGIN' AND PULLIN' IN MY GUT. BUT MOSTLY IT'S 'CUZ OF WHAT THAT FEELIN' TURNED INTO.

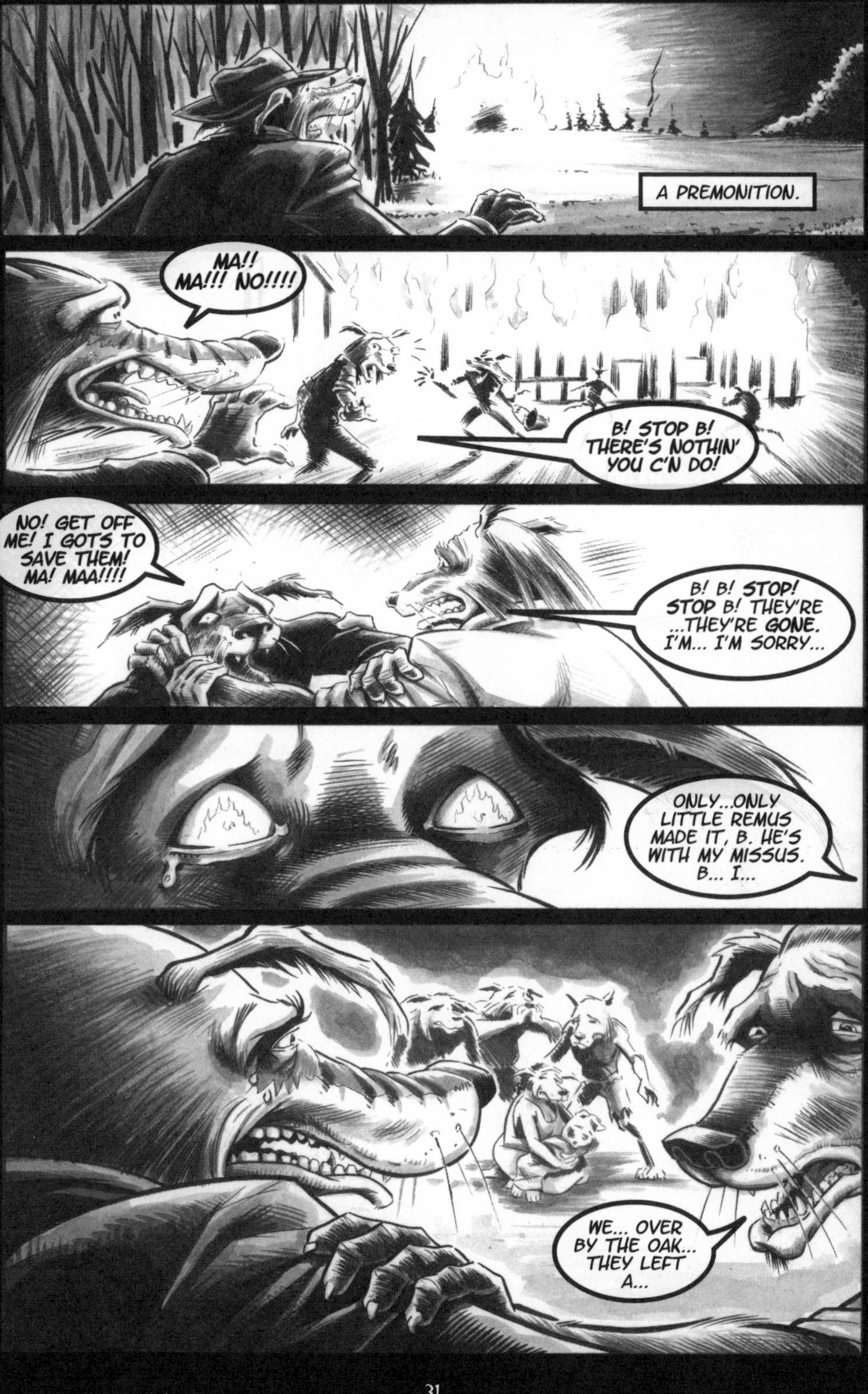

A PREMONITION.
MA!! MA!!! NO!!!!
B! STOP B! THERE'S NOTHIN' YOU C'N DO!
NO! GET OFF ME! I GOTS TO SAVE THEM! MA! MAA!!!!
B! B! STOP! STOP B! THEY'RE ...THEY'RE GONE. I'M... I'M SORRY...
ONLY...ONLY LITTLE REMUS MADE IT, B. HE'S WITH MY MISSUS. B... I...
WE... OVER BY THE OAK... THEY LEFT A...

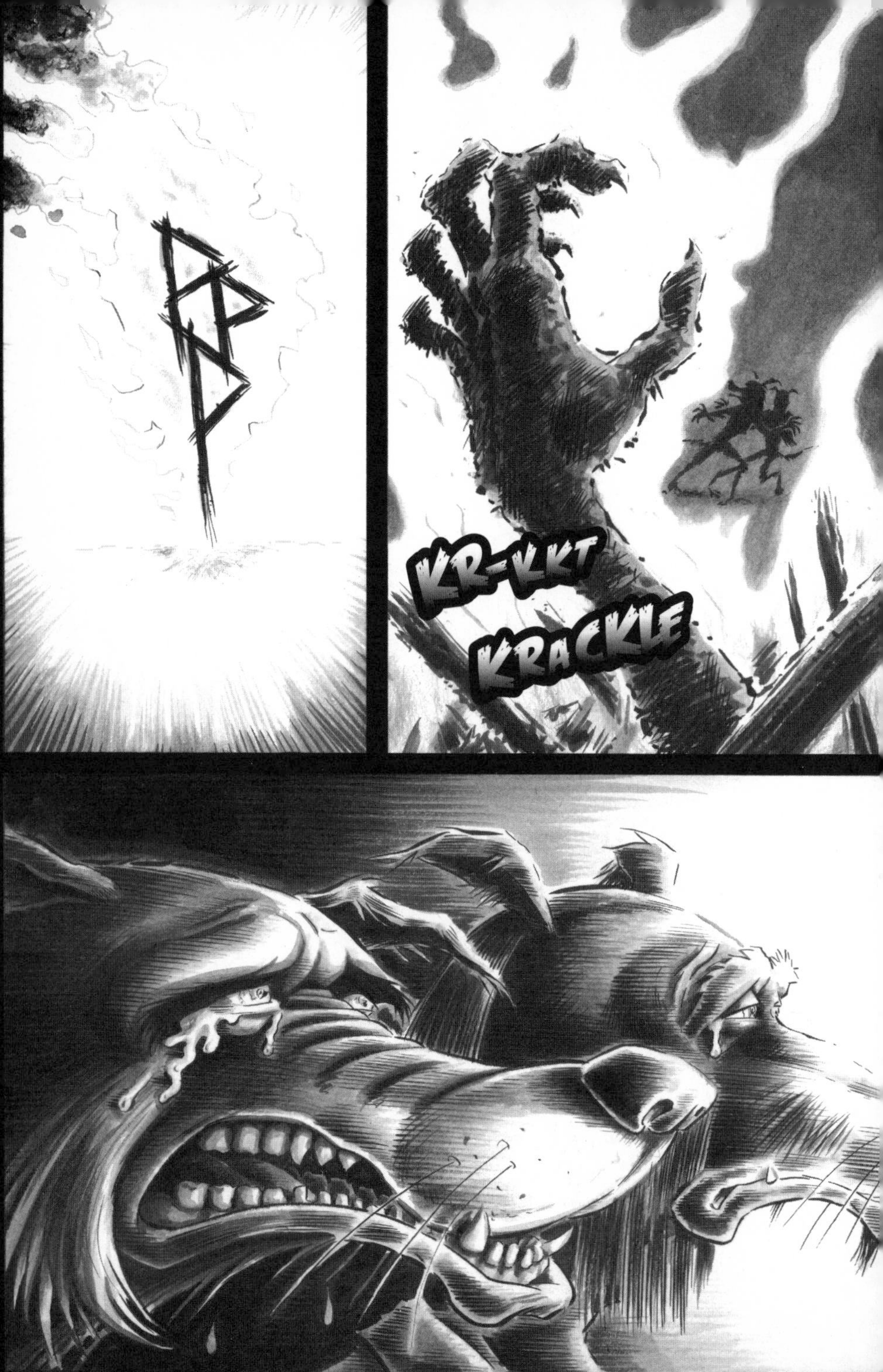
KR-KKT
KRACKLE

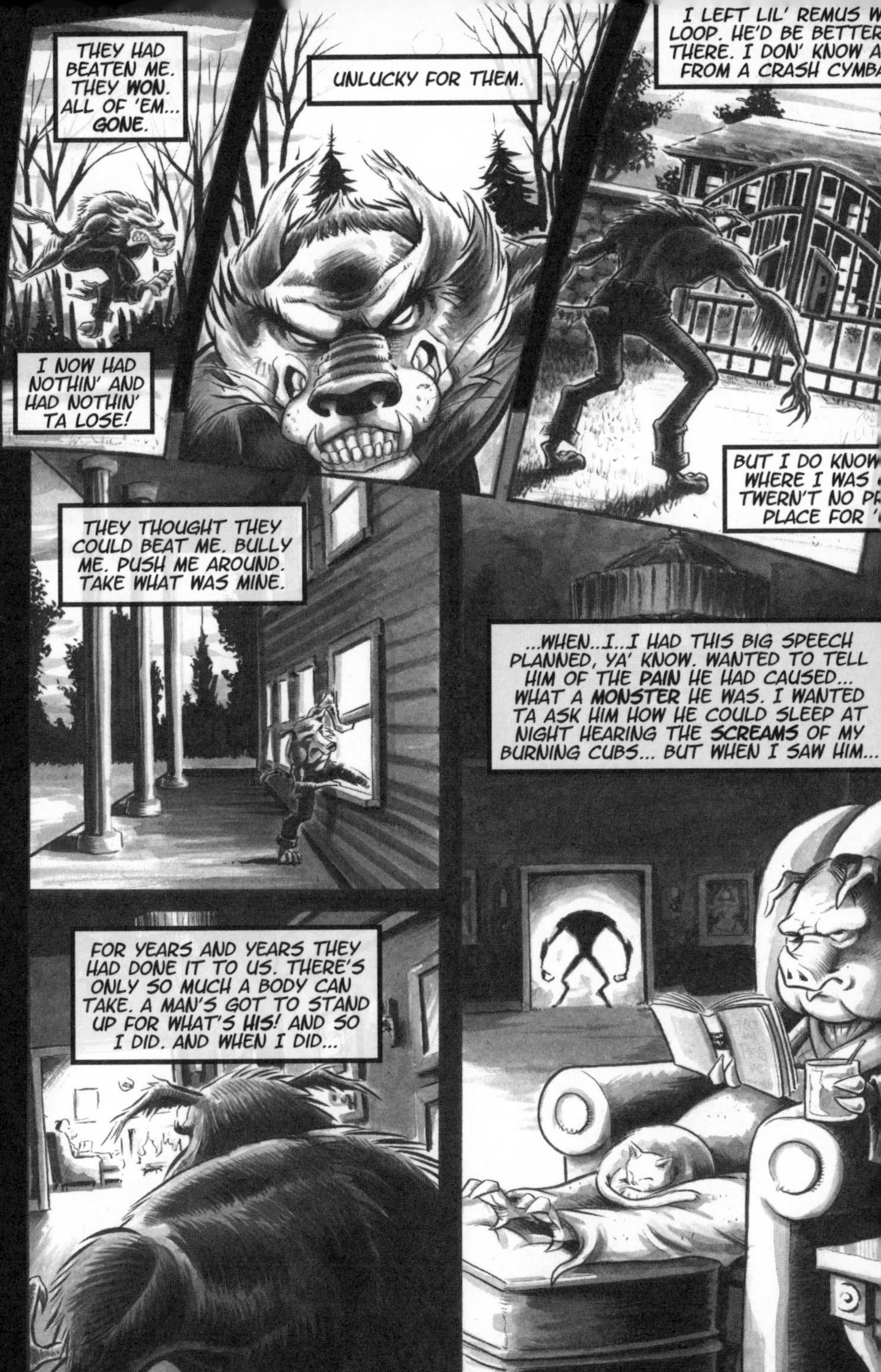
THEY HAD BEATEN ME. THEY WON. ALL OF 'EM... GONE.
I NOW HAD NOTHIN' AND HAD NOTHIN' TA LOSE!
UNLUCKY FOR THEM.
I LEFT LIL' REMUS
LOOP. HE'D BE BETTER
THERE. I DON' KNOW
FROM A CRASH
BUT I DO KNOW
WHERE I WAS
TWERN'T NO
PLACE FOR
THEY THOUGHT THEY COULD BEAT ME. BULLY ME. PUSH ME AROUND. TAKE WHAT WAS MINE.
FOR YEARS AND YEARS THEY HAD DONE IT TO US. THERE'S ONLY SO MUCH A BODY CAN TAKE. A MAN'S GOT TO STAND UP FOR WHAT'S HIS! AND SO I DID. AND WHEN I DID...
...WHEN...I...I HAD THIS BIG SPEECH PLANNED, YA' KNOW. WANTED TO TELL HIM OF THE PAIN HE HAD CAUSED... WHAT A MONSTER HE WAS. I WANTED TA ASK HIM HOW HE COULD SLEEP AT NIGHT HEARING THE SCREAMS OF MY BURNING CUBS... BUT WHEN I SAW HIM...

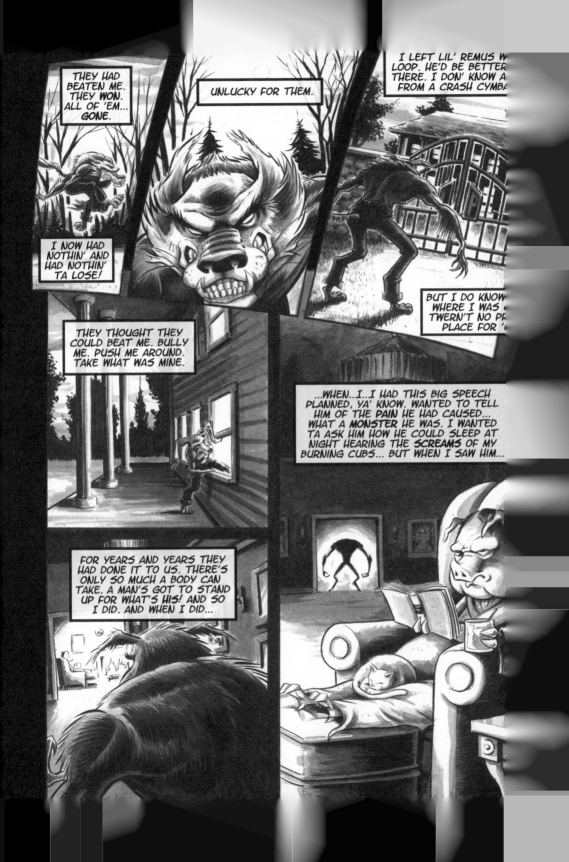

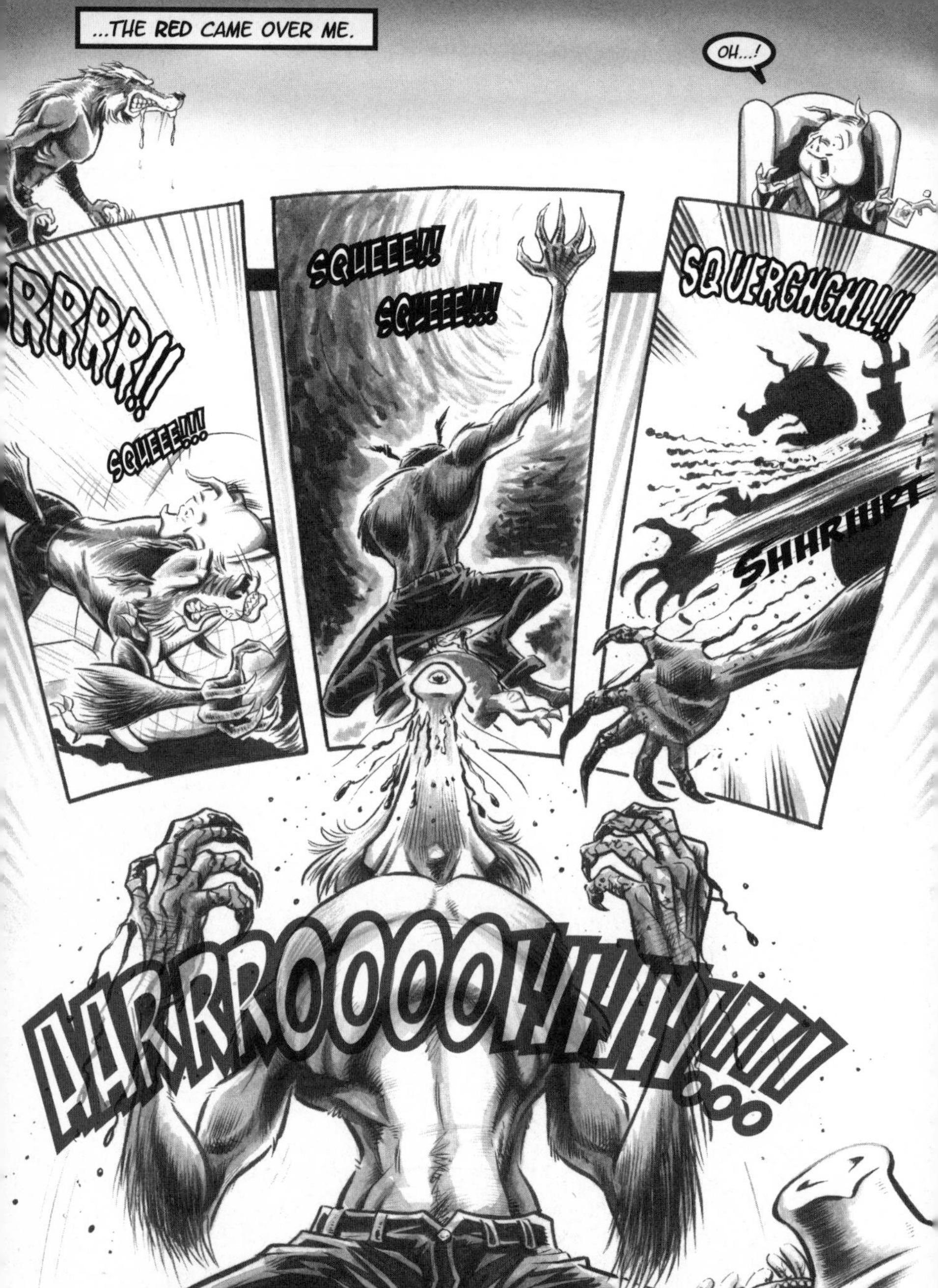

Oh, baby, the river's red.
Oh, baby, in my head.
—Led Zeppelin, *Four Sticks*

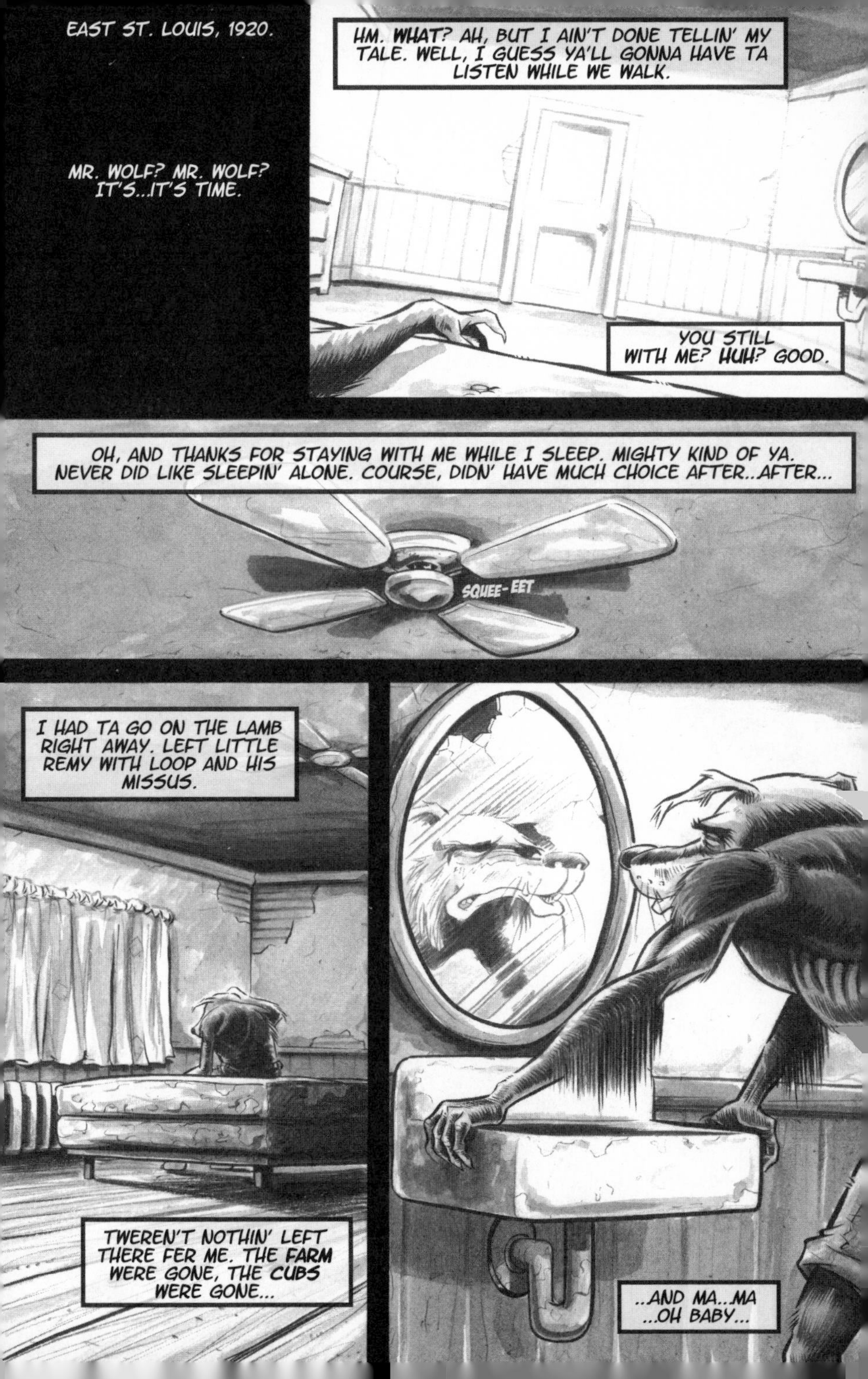

EAST ST. LOUIS, 1920.
MR. WOLF? MR. WOLF? IT'S...IT'S TIME.
HM. WHAT? AH, BUT I AIN'T DONE TELLIN' MY TALE. WELL, I GUESS YA'LL GONNA HAVE TA LISTEN WHILE WE WALK.
YOU STILL WITH ME? HUH? GOOD.
OH, AND THANKS FOR STAYING WITH ME WHILE I SLEEP. MIGHTY KIND OF YA. NEVER DID LIKE SLEEPIN' ALONE. COURSE, DIDN' HAVE MUCH CHOICE AFTER..AFTER...
SQUEE-EET
I HAD TA GO ON THE LAMB RIGHT AWAY. LEFT LITTLE REMY WITH LOOP AND HIS MISSUS.
TWEREN'T NOTHIN' LEFT THERE FER ME. THE FARM WERE GONE, THE CUBS WERE GONE...
..AND MA...MA ...OH BABY...

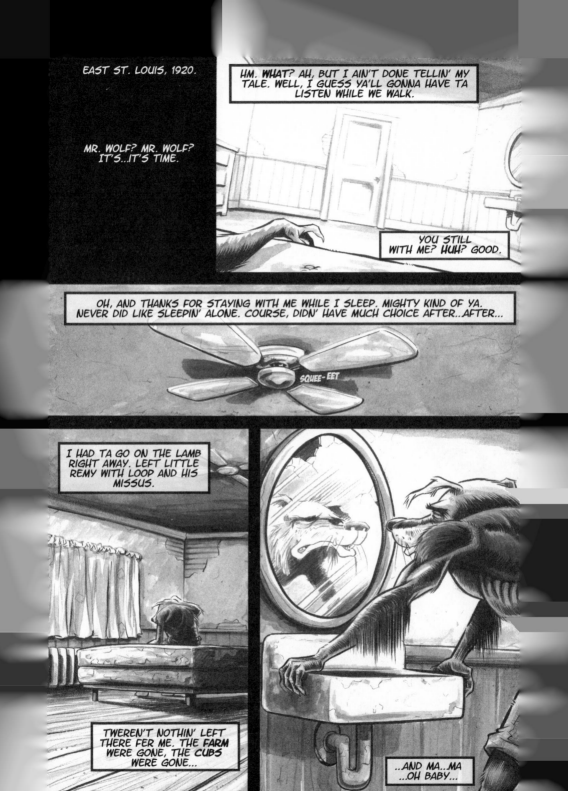

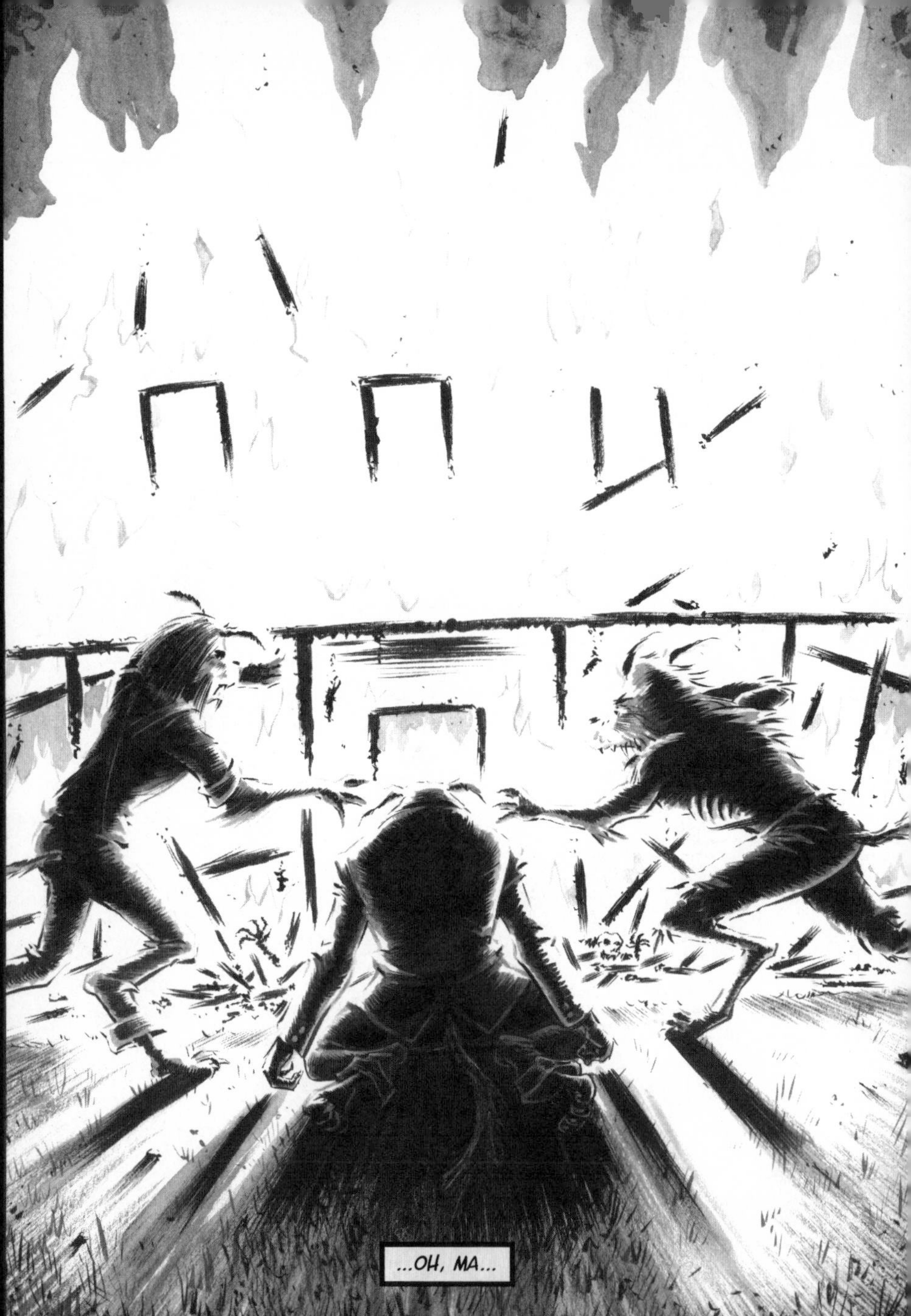
...OH, MA...

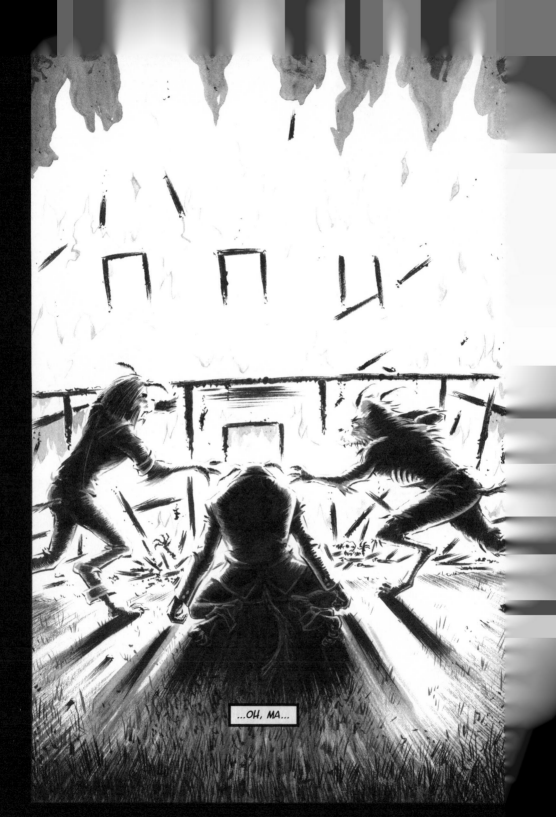

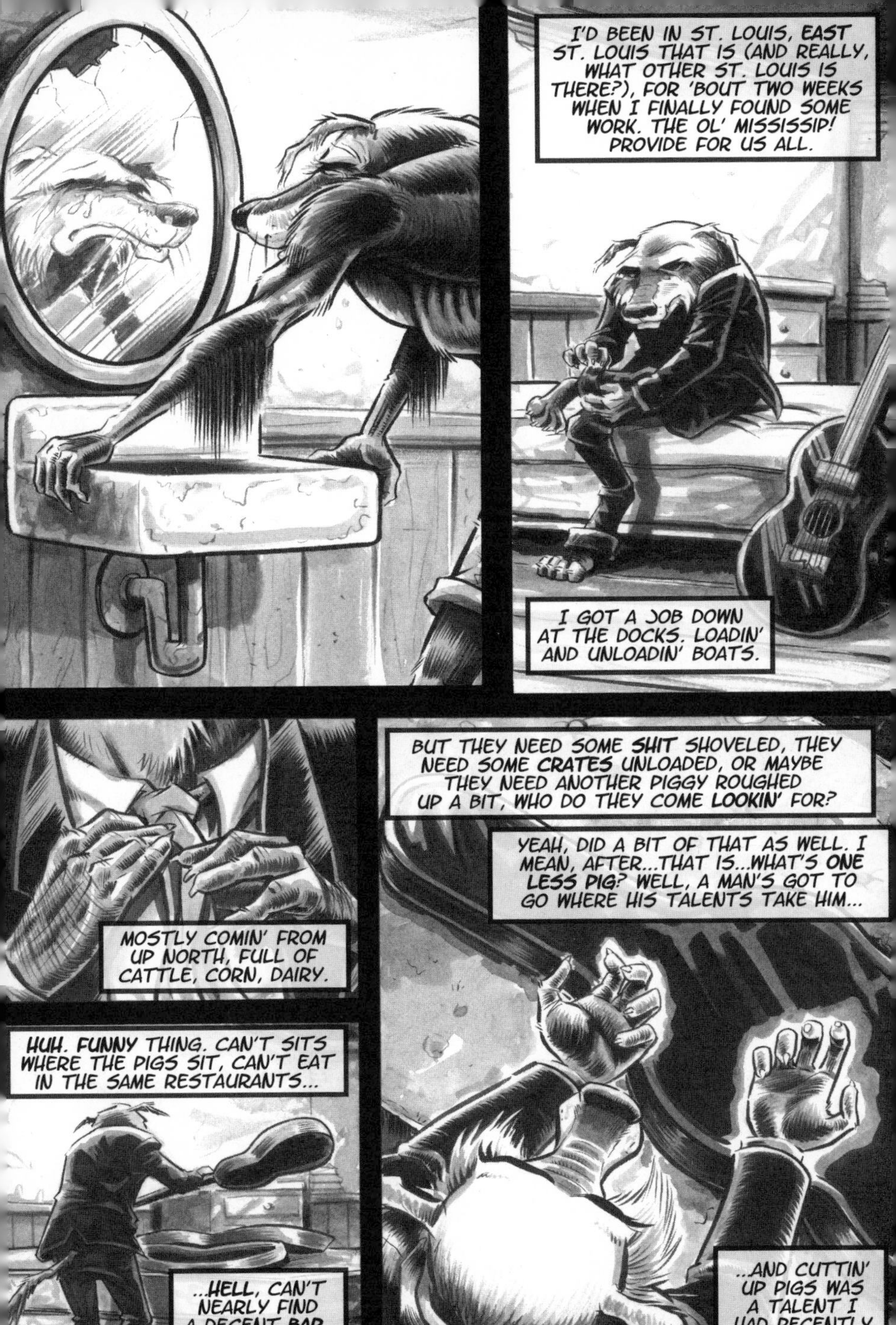
I'D BEEN IN ST. LOUIS, EAST ST. LOUIS THAT IS (AND REALLY, WHAT OTHER ST. LOUIS IS THERE?), FOR 'BOUT TWO WEEKS WHEN I FINALLY FOUND SOME WORK. THE OL' MISSISSIP! PROVIDE FOR US ALL.
I GOT A JOB DOWN AT THE DOCKS. LOADIN' AND UNLOADIN' BOATS.
MOSTLY COMIN' FROM UP NORTH, FULL OF CATTLE, CORN, DAIRY.
HUH. FUNNY THING. CAN'T SITS WHERE THE PIGS SIT, CAN'T EAT IN THE SAME RESTAURANTS...
...HELL, CAN'T NEARLY FIND A DECENT BAR THAT'LL SERVE US WOLVES.
BUT THEY NEED SOME SHIT SHOVELED, THEY NEED SOME CRATES UNLOADED, OR MAYBE THEY NEED ANOTHER PIGGY ROUGHED UP A BIT, WHO DO THEY COME LOOKIN' FOR?
YEAH, DID A BIT OF THAT AS WELL. I MEAN, AFTER...THAT IS...WHAT'S ONE LESS PIG? WELL, A MAN'S GOT TO GO WHERE HIS TALENTS TAKE HIM...
...AND CUTTIN' UP PIGS WAS A TALENT I HAD RECENTLY DISCOVERED.

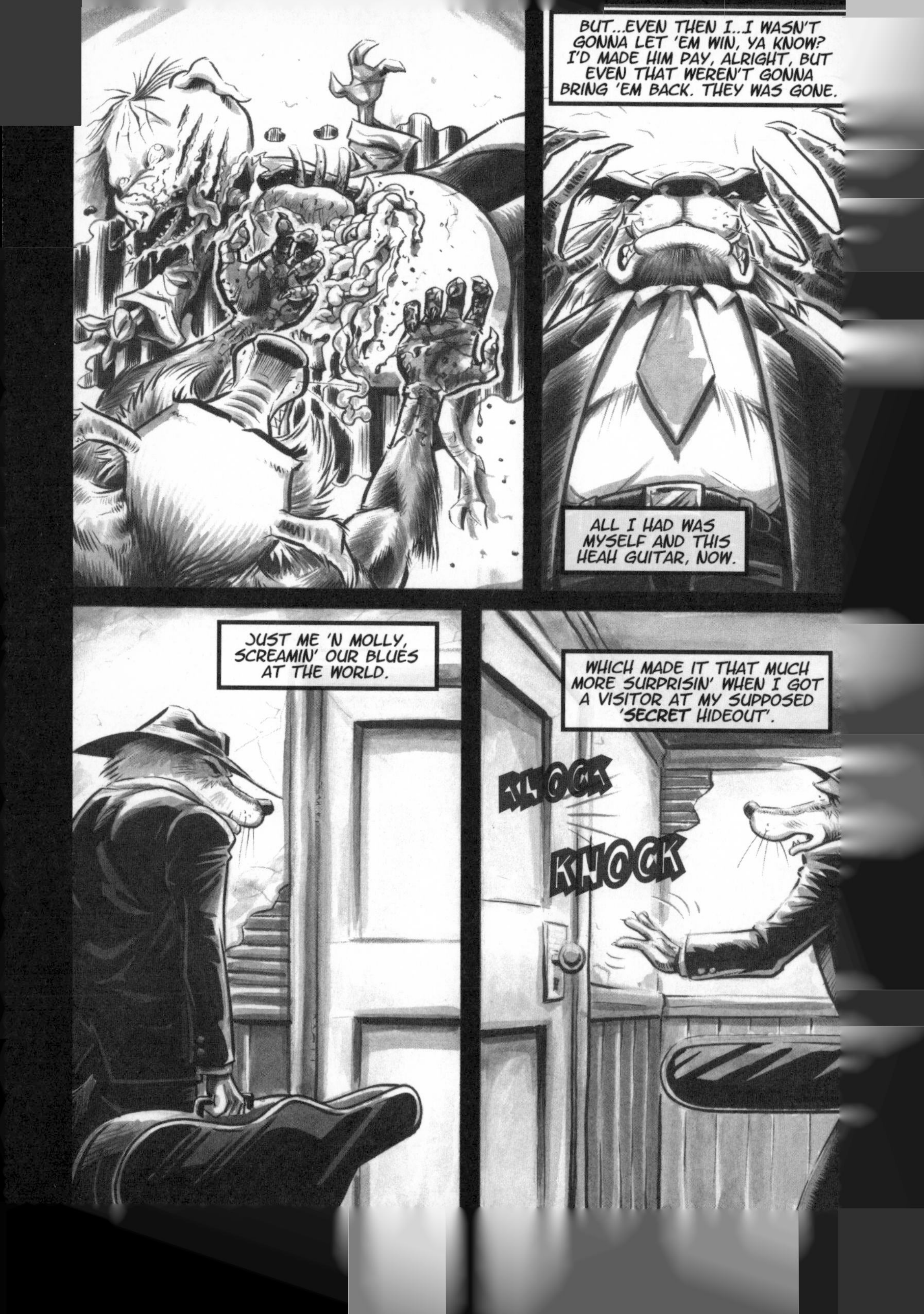
BUT...EVEN THEN I...I WASN'T GONNA LET 'EM WIN, YA KNOW? I'D MADE HIM PAY, ALRIGHT, BUT EVEN THAT WEREN'T GONNA BRING 'EM BACK. THEY WAS GONE.
ALL I HAD WAS MYSELF AND THIS HEAH GUITAR, NOW.
JUST ME 'N MOLLY, SCREAMIN' OUR BLUES AT THE WORLD.
WHICH MADE IT THAT MUCH MORE SURPRISIN' WHEN I GOT A VISITOR AT MY SUPPOSED 'SECRET HIDEOUT'.
KNOCK
KNOCK

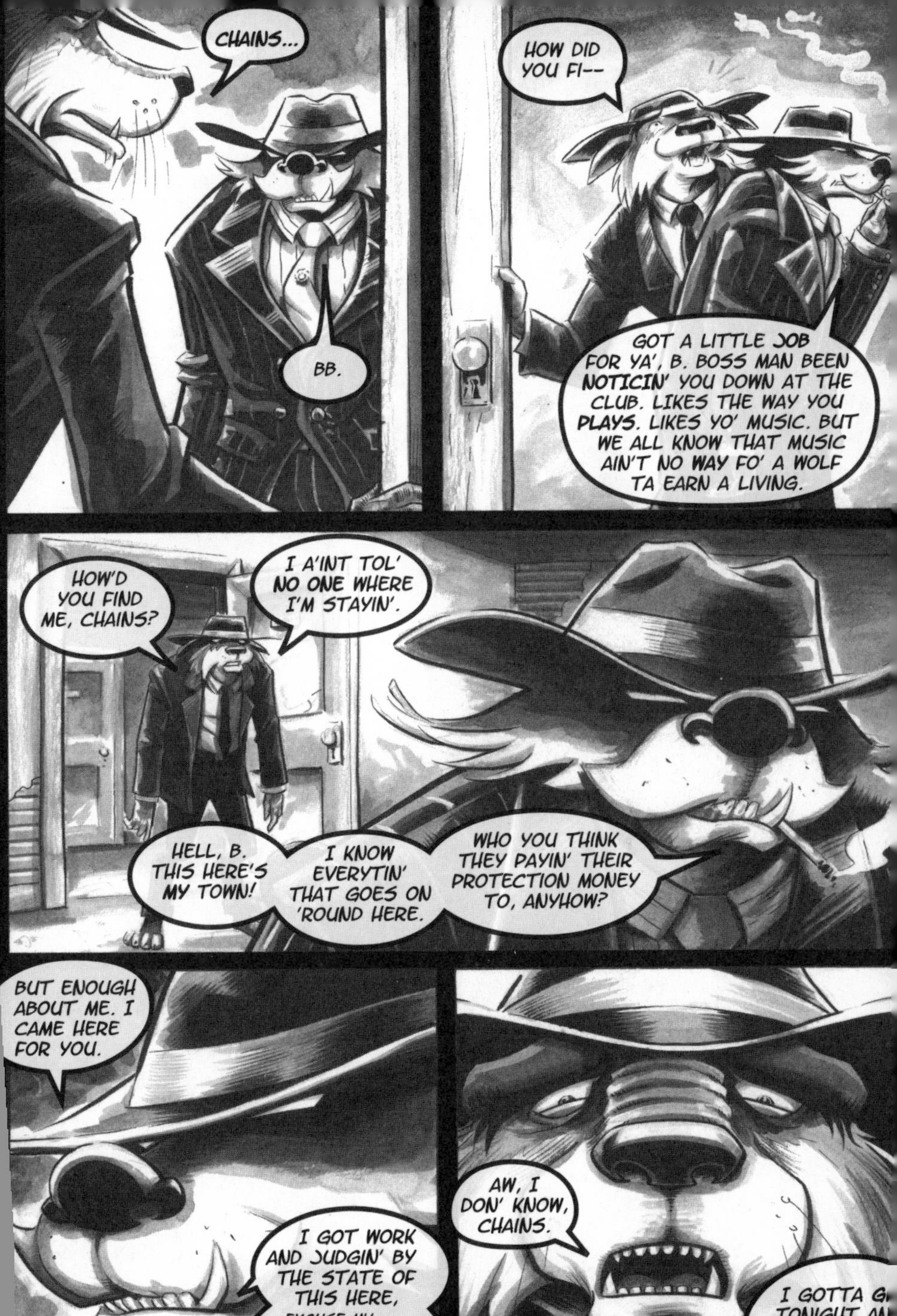
CHAINS...
BB.
HOW DID YOU FI--
GOT A LITTLE JOB FOR YA', B. BOSS MAN BEEN NOTICIN' YOU DOWN AT THE CLUB. LIKES THE WAY YOU PLAYS. LIKES YO' MUSIC. BUT WE ALL KNOW THAT MUSIC AIN'T NO WAY FO' A WOLF TA EARN A LIVING.
HOW'D YOU FIND ME, CHAINS?
I A'INT TOL' NO ONE WHERE I'M STAYIN'.
HELL, B. THIS HERE'S MY TOWN!
I KNOW EVERYTIN' THAT GOES ON 'ROUND HERE.
WHO YOU THINK THEY PAYIN' THEIR PROTECTION MONEY TO, ANYHOW?
BUT ENOUGH ABOUT ME. I CAME HERE FOR YOU.
I GOT WORK AND JUDGIN' BY THE STATE OF THIS HERE, EXCUSE MY FRENCH, PIGSTY, YOU NEED IT. NOW, YOU INTERESTED?
AW, I DON' KNOW, CHAINS.
I GOTTA G
TONIGHT AN
I'M ALREAD
PRETTY BEA
MAYBE..

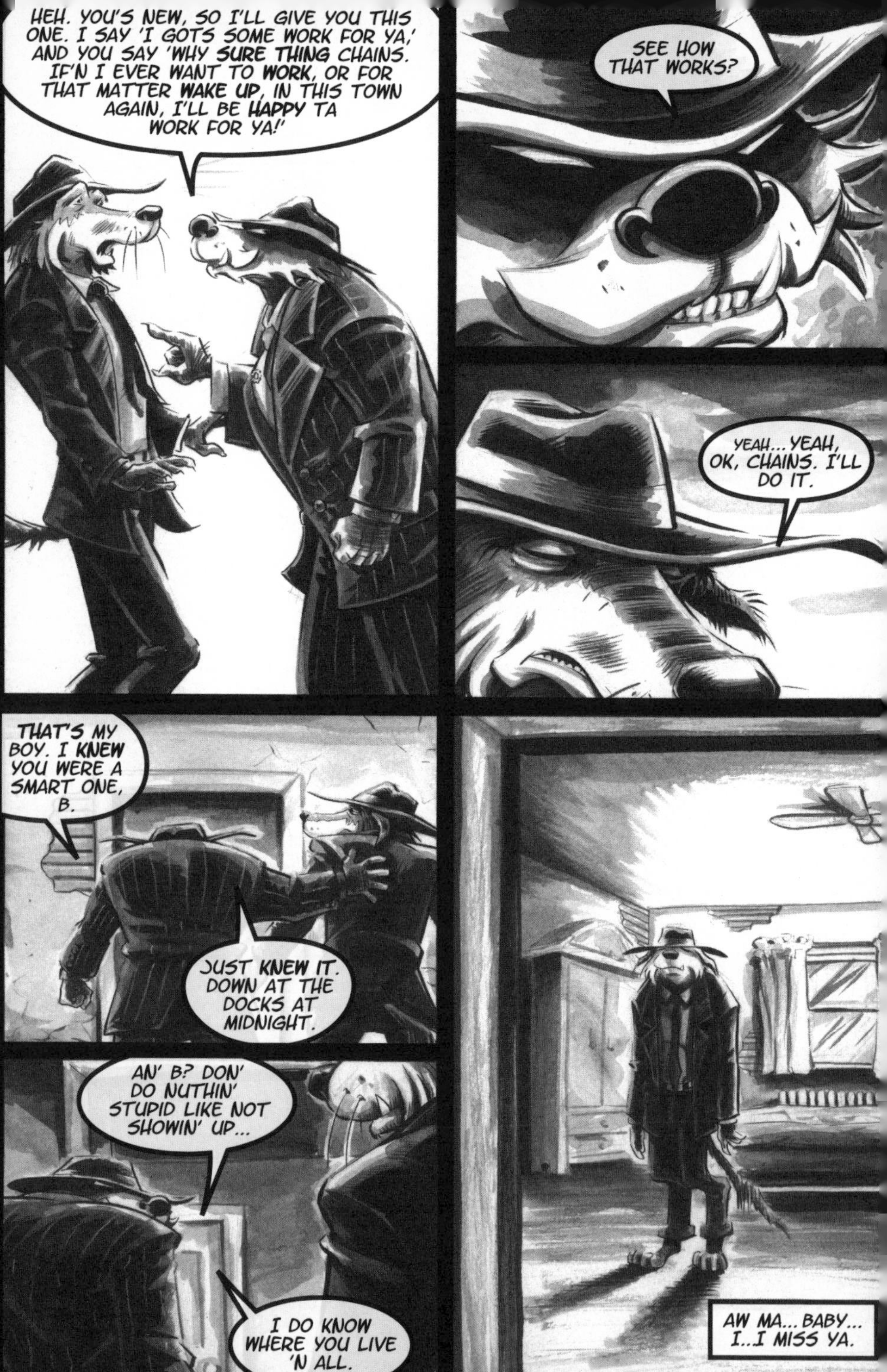
HEH. YOU'S NEW, SO I'LL GIVE YOU THIS ONE. I SAY 'I GOTS SOME WORK FOR YA,' AND YOU SAY 'WHY SURE THING CHAINS. IF'N I EVER WANT TO WORK, OR FOR THAT MATTER WAKE UP, IN THIS TOWN AGAIN, I'LL BE HAPPY TA WORK FOR YA!'
SEE HOW THAT WORKS?
YEAH... YEAH, OK, CHAINS. I'LL DO IT.
THAT'S MY BOY. I KNEW YOU WERE A SMART ONE, B.
JUST KNEW IT. DOWN AT THE DOCKS AT MIDNIGHT.
AN' B? DON' DO NUTHIN' STUPID LIKE NOT SHOWIN' UP...
I DO KNOW WHERE YOU LIVE 'N ALL.
AW MA... BABY... I...I MISS YA.

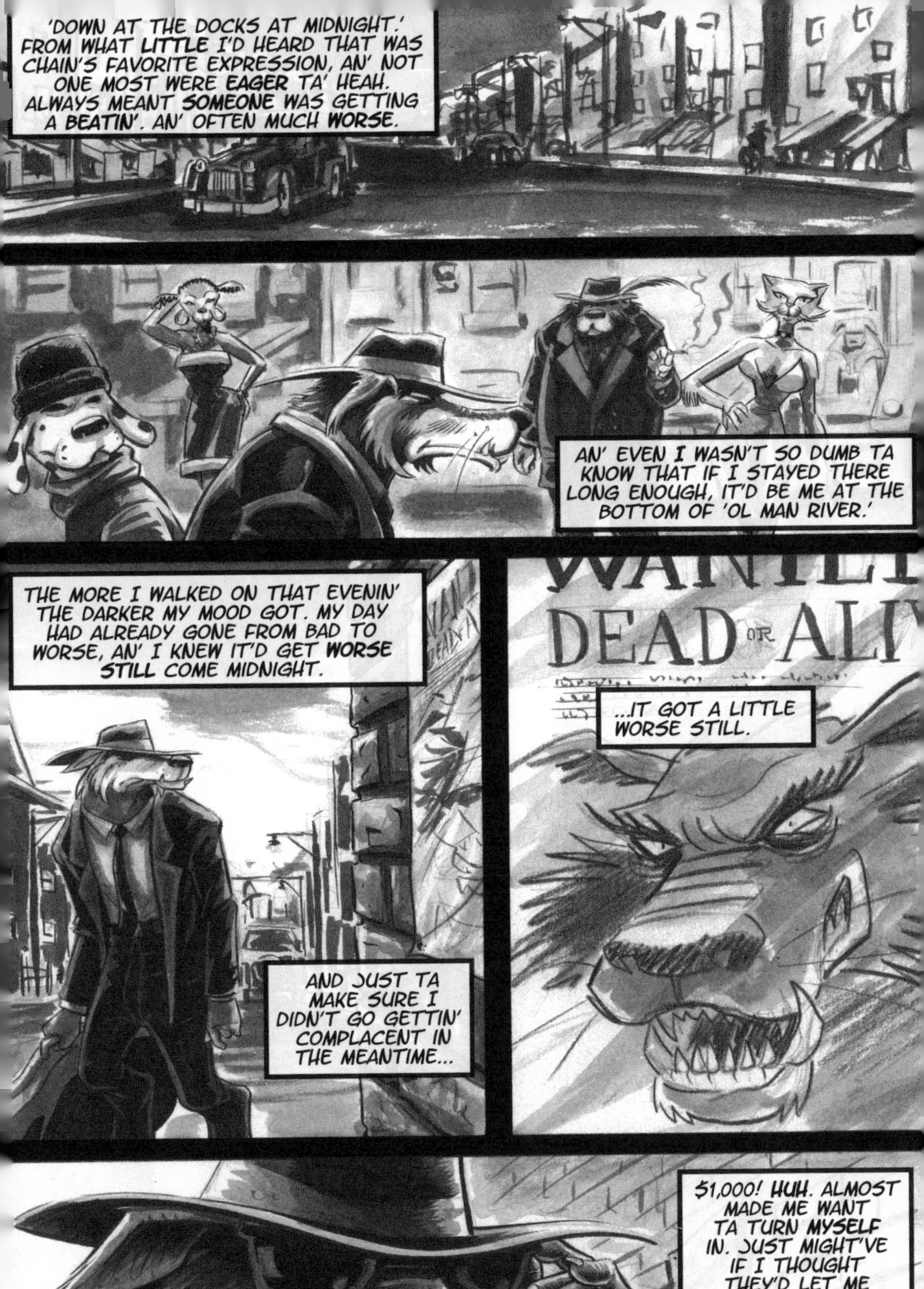

'DOWN AT THE DOCKS AT MIDNIGHT.' FROM WHAT LITTLE I'D HEARD THAT WAS CHAIN'S FAVORITE EXPRESSION, AN' NOT ONE MOST WERE EAGER TA' HEAH. ALWAYS MEANT SOMEONE WAS GETTING A BEATIN'. AN' OFTEN MUCH WORSE.
AN' EVEN I WASN'T SO DUMB TA KNOW THAT IF I STAYED THERE LONG ENOUGH, IT'D BE ME AT THE BOTTOM OF 'OL MAN RIVER.'
THE MORE I WALKED ON THAT EVENIN' THE DARKER MY MOOD GOT. MY DAY HAD ALREADY GONE FROM BAD TO WORSE, AN' I KNEW IT'D GET WORSE STILL COME MIDNIGHT.
AND JUST TA MAKE SURE I DIDN'T GO GETTIN' COMPLACENT IN THE MEANTIME...
DEAD OR ALI
...IT GOT A LITTLE WORSE STILL.
$1,000! HUH. ALMOST MADE ME WANT TA TURN MYSELF IN. JUST MIGHT'VE IF I THOUGHT THEY'D LET ME SPEND THE MONEY FIRST.

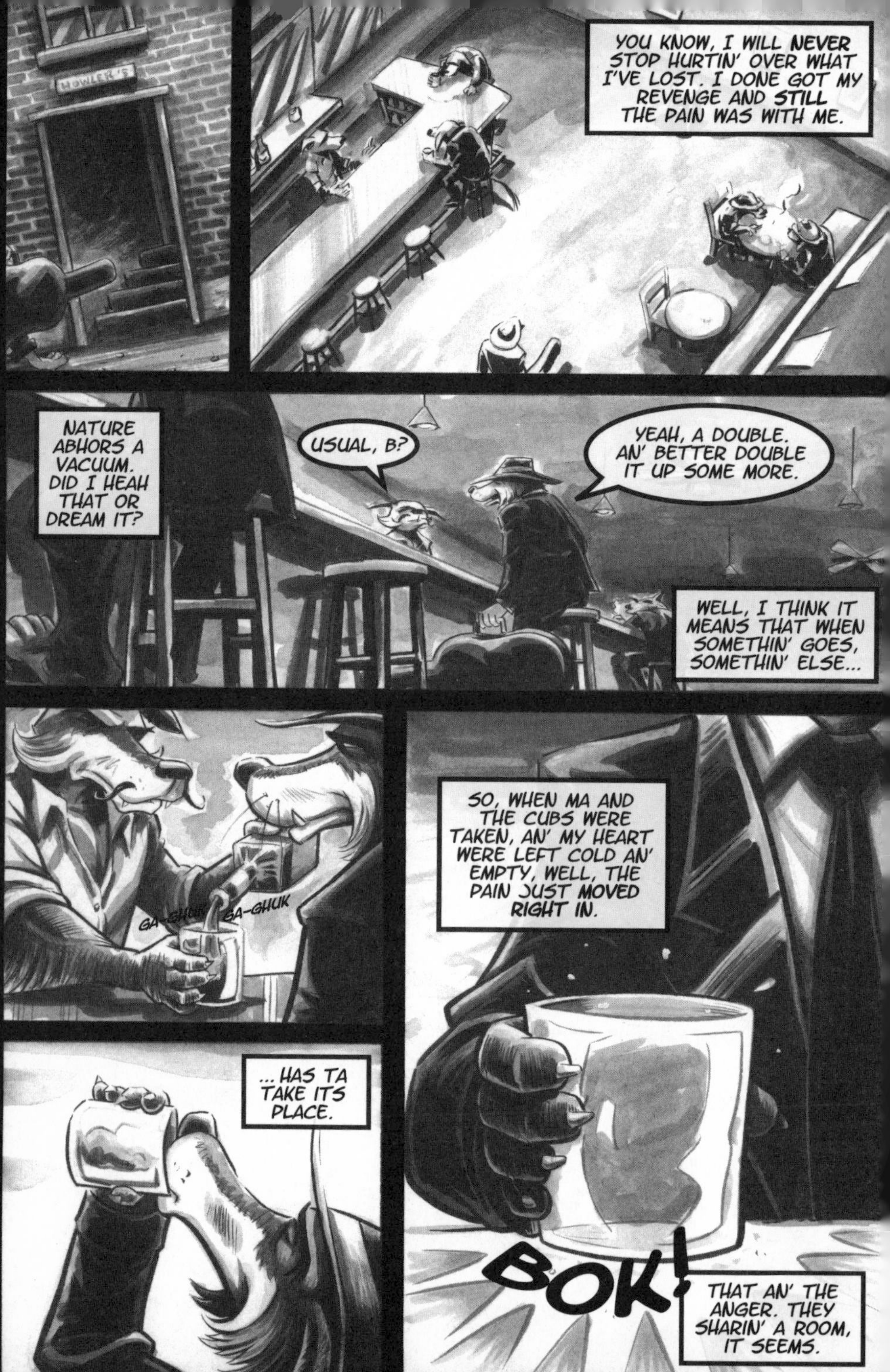
HOWLER'S
YOU KNOW, I WILL NEVER STOP HURTIN' OVER WHAT I'VE LOST. I DONE GOT MY REVENGE AND STILL THE PAIN WAS WITH ME.
NATURE ABHORS A VACUUM. DID I HEAH THAT OR DREAM IT?
USUAL, B?
YEAH, A DOUBLE. AN' BETTER DOUBLE IT UP SOME MORE.
WELL, I THINK IT MEANS THAT WHEN SOMETHIN' GOES, SOMETHIN' ELSE...
GA-GHUK GA-GHUK
SO, WHEN MA AND THE CUBS WERE TAKEN, AN' MY HEART WERE LEFT COLD AN' EMPTY, WELL, THE PAIN JUST MOVED RIGHT IN.
...HAS TA TAKE ITS PLACE.
BOK!
THAT AN' THE ANGER. THEY SHARIN' A ROOM, IT SEEMS.

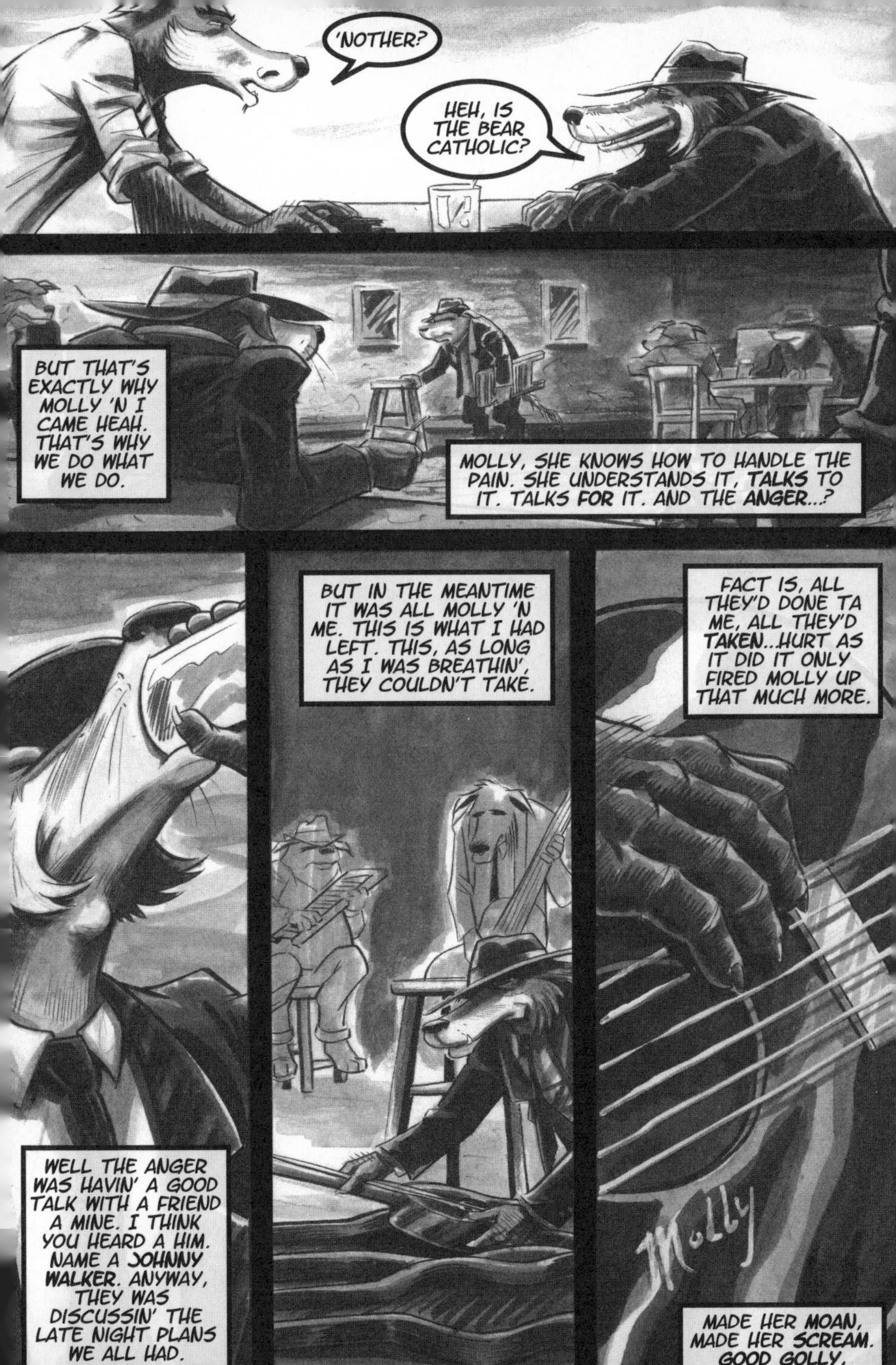
'NOTHER?
HEH, IS THE BEAR CATHOLIC?
BUT THAT'S EXACTLY WHY MOLLY 'N I CAME HEAH. THAT'S WHY WE DO WHAT WE DO.
MOLLY, SHE KNOWS HOW TO HANDLE THE PAIN. SHE UNDERSTANDS IT, TALKS TO IT. TALKS FOR IT. AND THE ANGER...?
WELL THE ANGER WAS HAVIN' A GOOD TALK WITH A FRIEND A MINE. I THINK YOU HEARD A HIM. NAME A JOHNNY WALKER. ANYWAY, THEY WAS DISCUSSIN' THE LATE NIGHT PLANS WE ALL HAD.
BUT IN THE MEANTIME IT WAS ALL MOLLY 'N ME. THIS IS WHAT I HAD LEFT. THIS, AS LONG AS I WAS BREATHIN', THEY COULDN'T TAKE.
FACT IS, ALL THEY'D DONE TA ME, ALL THEY'D TAKEN...HURT AS IT DID IT ONLY FIRED MOLLY UP THAT MUCH MORE.
Molly
MADE HER MOAN, MADE HER SCREAM. GOOD GOLLY, MISS MOLLY...

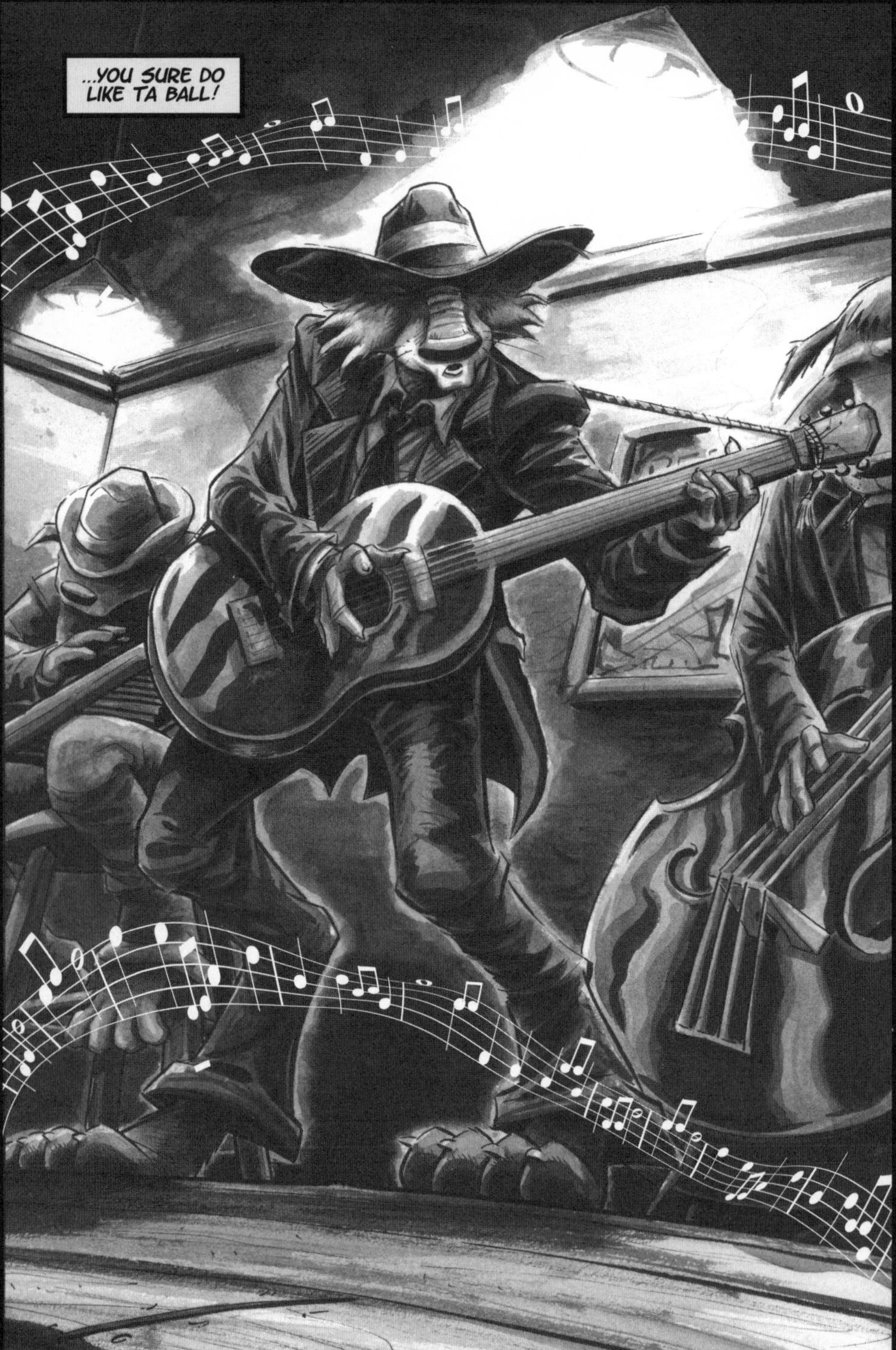
...YOU SURE DO
LIKE TA BALL!

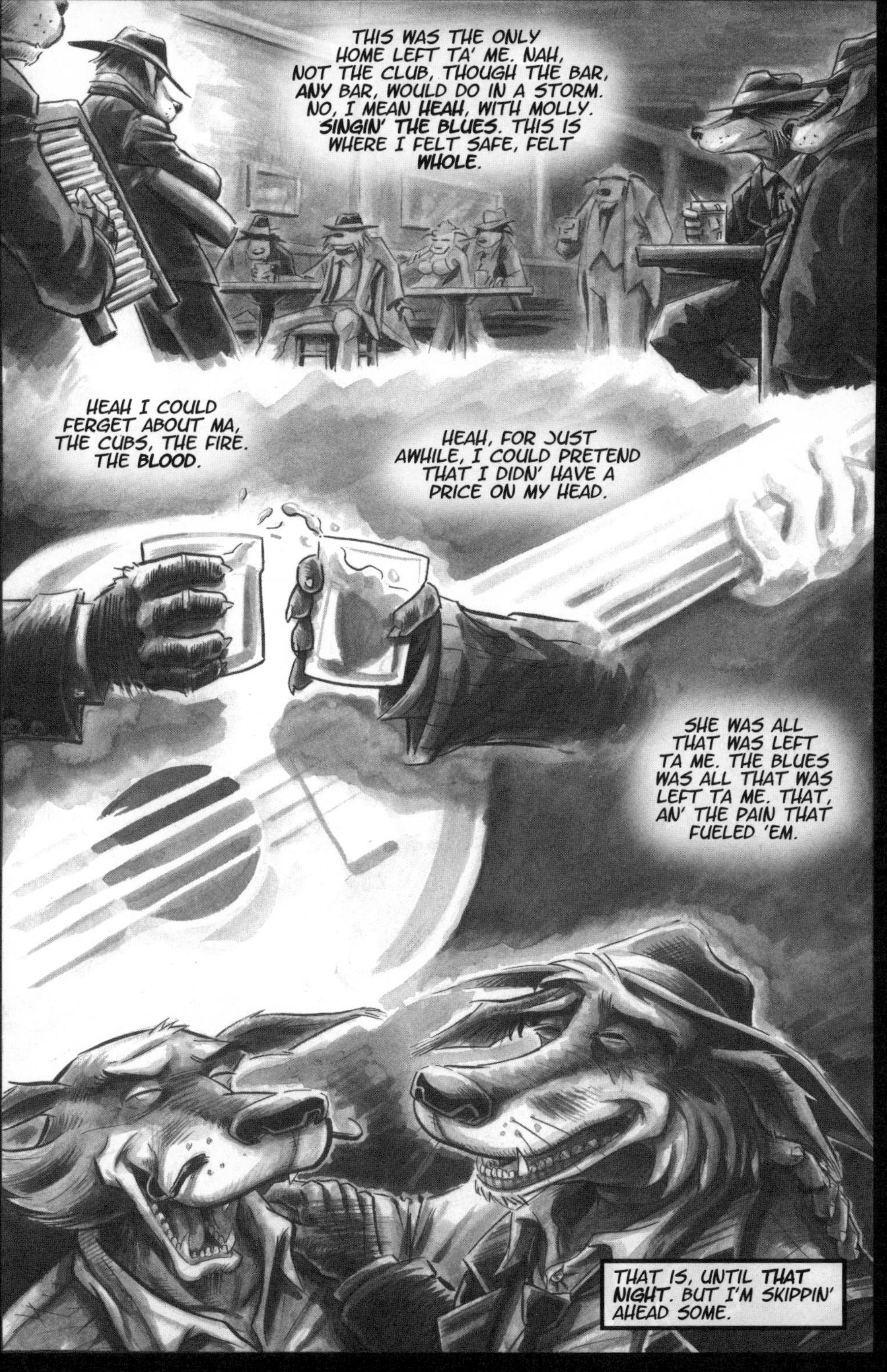
THIS WAS THE ONLY HOME LEFT TA' ME. NAH, NOT THE CLUB, THOUGH THE BAR, ANY BAR, WOULD DO IN A STORM. NO, I MEAN HEAH, WITH MOLLY. SINGIN' THE BLUES. THIS IS WHERE I FELT SAFE, FELT WHOLE.
HEAH I COULD FERGET ABOUT MA, THE CUBS, THE FIRE. THE BLOOD.
HEAH, FOR JUST AWHILE, I COULD PRETEND THAT I DIDN' HAVE A PRICE ON MY HEAD.
SHE WAS ALL THAT WAS LEFT TA ME. THE BLUES WAS ALL THAT WAS LEFT TA ME. THAT, AN' THE PAIN THAT FUELED 'EM.
THAT IS, UNTIL THAT NIGHT. BUT I'M SKIPPIN' AHEAD SOME.

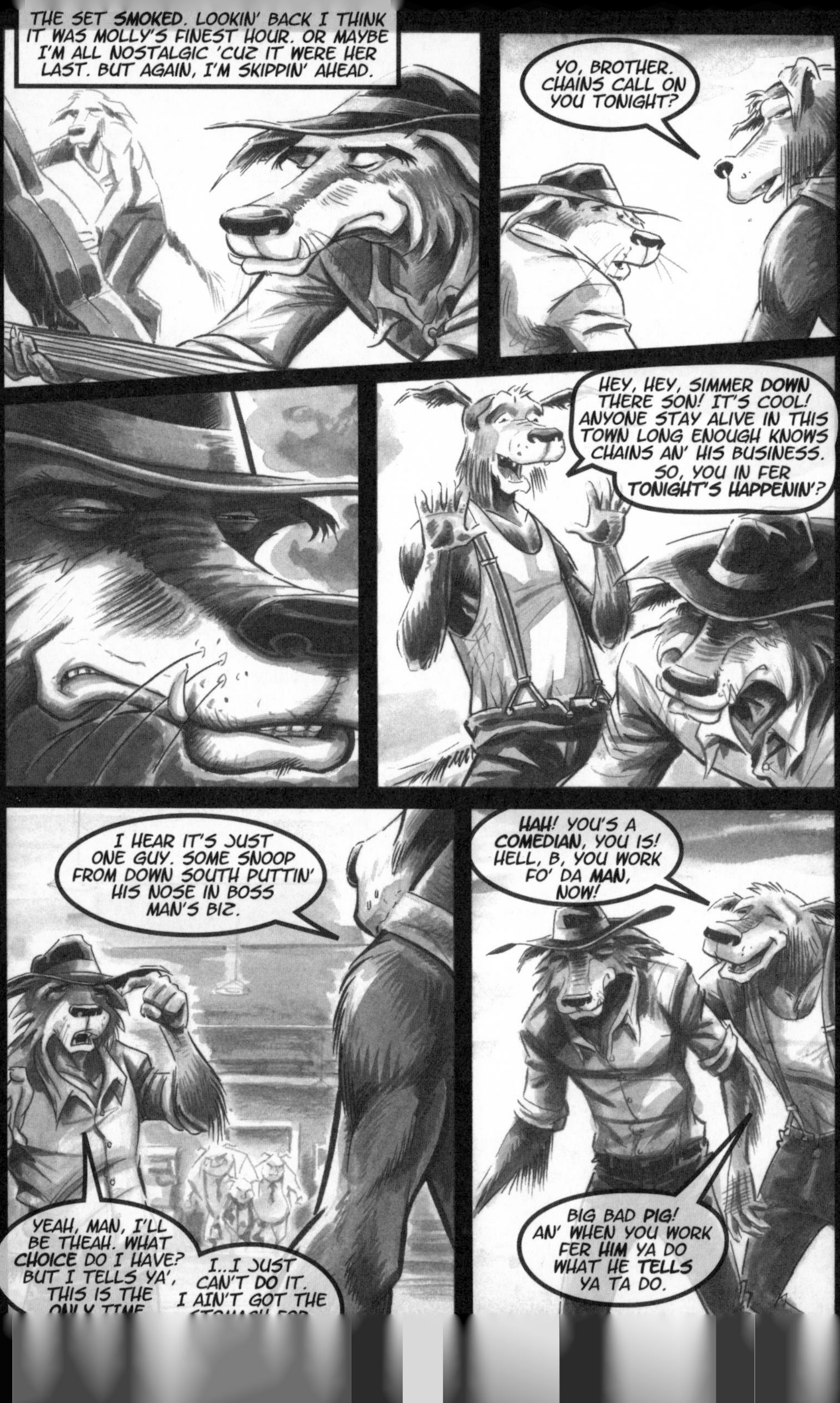
THE SET SMOKED. LOOKIN' BACK I THINK IT WAS MOLLY'S FINEST HOUR. OR MAYBE I'M ALL NOSTALGIC 'CUZ IT WERE HER LAST. BUT AGAIN, I'M SKIPPIN' AHEAD.
YO, BROTHER. CHAINS CALL ON YOU TONIGHT?
HEY, HEY, SIMMER DOWN THERE SON! IT'S COOL! ANYONE STAY ALIVE IN THIS TOWN LONG ENOUGH KNOWS CHAINS AN' HIS BUSINESS. SO, YOU IN FER TONIGHT'S HAPPENIN'?
I HEAR IT'S JUST ONE GUY. SOME SNOOP FROM DOWN SOUTH PUTTIN' HIS NOSE IN BOSS MAN'S BIZ.
YEAH, MAN, I'LL BE THEAH. WHAT CHOICE DO I HAVE? BUT I TELLS YA', THIS IS THE
I...I JUST CAN'T DO IT. I AIN'T GOT THE
HAH! YOU'S A COMEDIAN, YOU IS! HELL, B, YOU WORK FO' DA MAN, NOW!
BIG BAD PIG! AN' WHEN YOU WORK FER HIM YA DO WHAT HE TELLS YA TA DO.

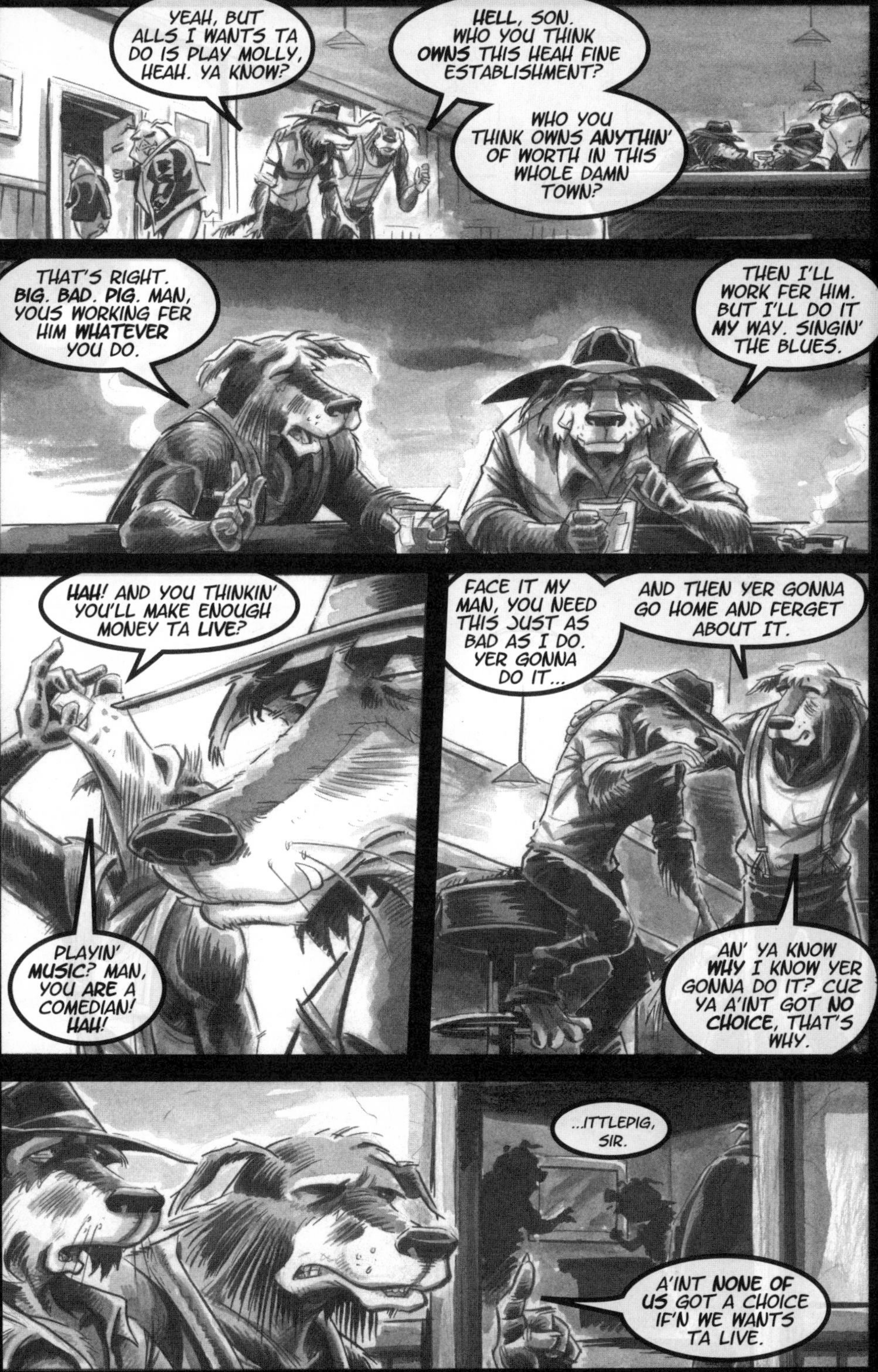

YEAH, BUT ALLS I WANTS TA DO IS PLAY MOLLY, HEAH. YA KNOW?
HELL, SON. WHO YOU THINK OWNS THIS HEAH FINE ESTABLISHMENT?
WHO YOU THINK OWNS ANYTHIN' OF WORTH IN THIS WHOLE DAMN TOWN?
THAT'S RIGHT. BIG. BAD. PIG. MAN, YOUS WORKING FER HIM WHATEVER YOU DO.
THEN I'LL WORK FER HIM. BUT I'LL DO IT MY WAY. SINGIN' THE BLUES.
HAH! AND YOU THINKIN' YOU'LL MAKE ENOUGH MONEY TA LIVE?
PLAYIN' MUSIC? MAN, YOU ARE A COMEDIAN! HAH!
FACE IT MY MAN, YOU NEED THIS JUST AS BAD AS I DO. YER GONNA DO IT...
AND THEN YER GONNA GO HOME AND FERGET ABOUT IT.
AN' YA KNOW WHY I KNOW YER GONNA DO IT? CUZ YA A'INT GOT NO CHOICE, THAT'S WHY.
...ITTLEPIG, SIR.
A'INT NONE OF US GOT A CHOICE IF'N WE WANTS TA LIVE.

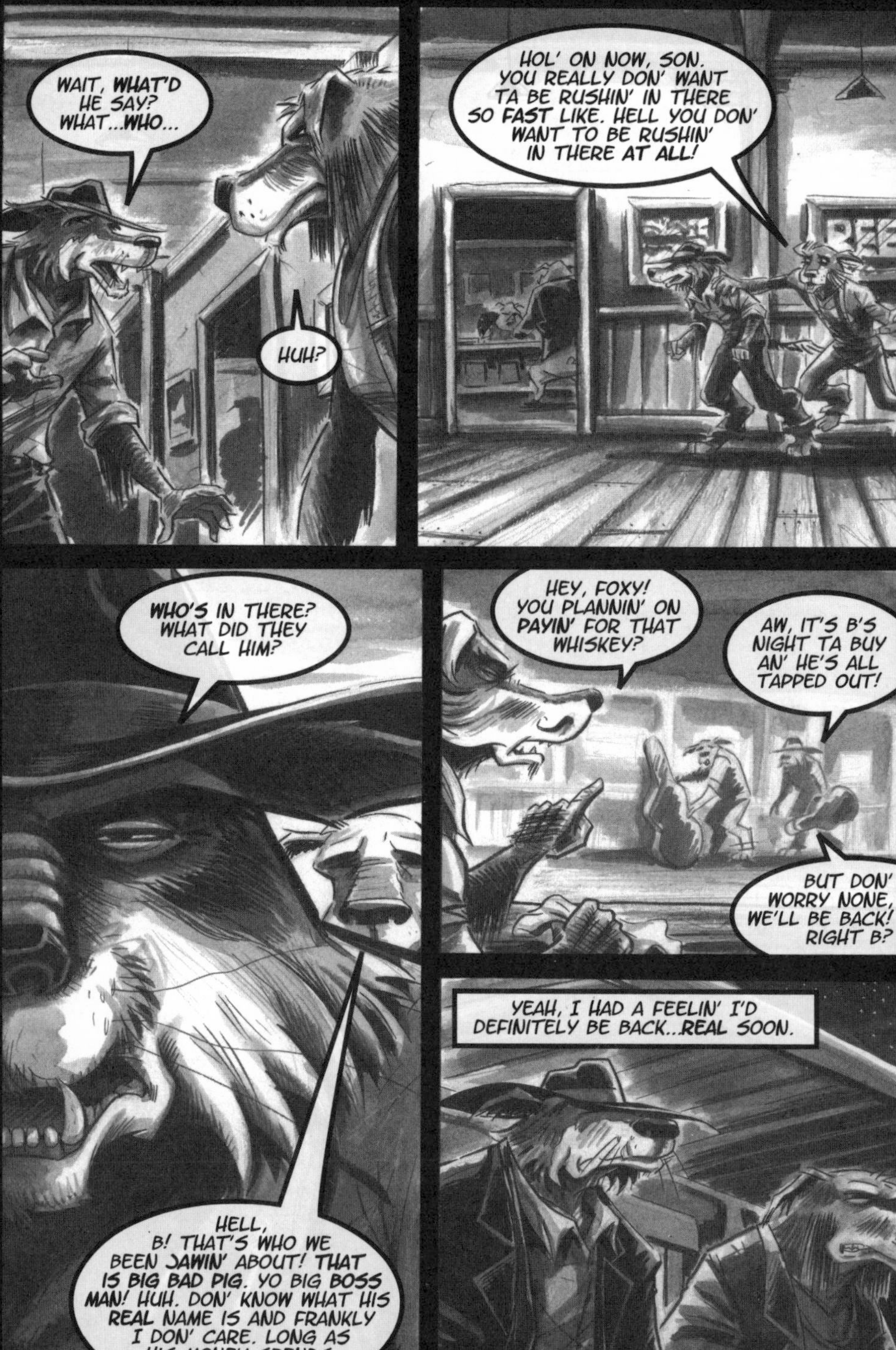
WAIT, WHAT'D HE SAY? WHAT...WHO...
HUH?
HOL' ON NOW, SON. YOU REALLY DON' WANT TA BE RUSHIN' IN THERE SO FAST LIKE. HELL YOU DON' WANT TO BE RUSHIN' IN THERE AT ALL!
WHO'S IN THERE? WHAT DID THEY CALL HIM?
HELL, B! THAT'S WHO WE BEEN JAWIN' ABOUT! THAT IS BIG BAD PIG. YO BIG BOSS MAN! HUH. DON' KNOW WHAT HIS REAL NAME IS AND FRANKLY I DON' CARE. LONG AS HIS MONEY SPENDS, YA GET ME?
HEY, FOXY! YOU PLANNIN' ON PAYIN' FOR THAT WHISKEY?
AW, IT'S B'S NIGHT TA BUY AN' HE'S ALL TAPPED OUT!
BUT DON' WORRY NONE, WE'LL BE BACK! RIGHT B?
YEAH, I HAD A FEELIN' I'D DEFINITELY BE BACK...REAL SOON.

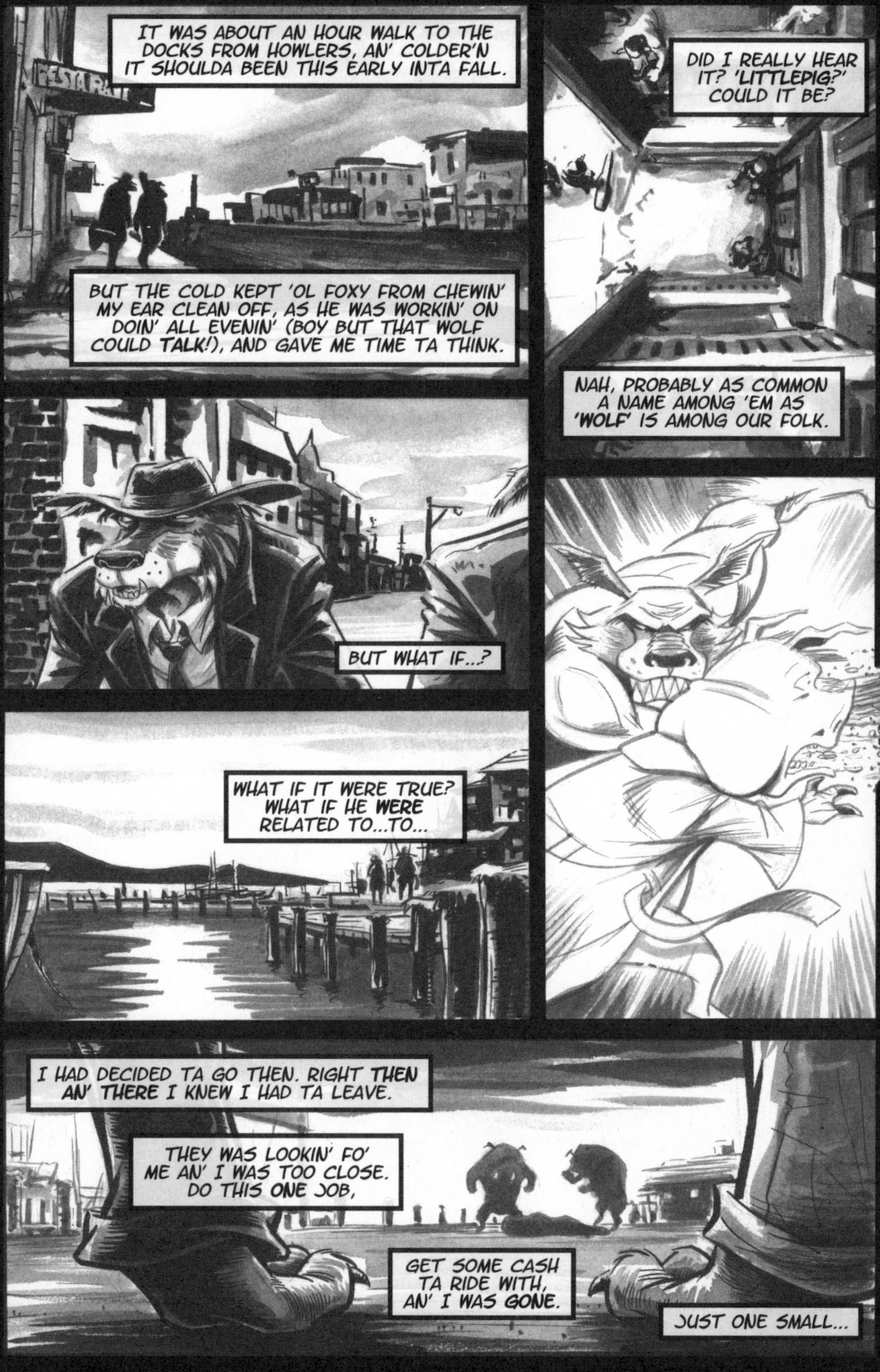

IT WAS ABOUT AN HOUR WALK TO THE DOCKS FROM HOWLERS, AN' COLDER'N IT SHOULDA BEEN THIS EARLY INTA FALL.
BUT THE COLD KEPT 'OL FOXY FROM CHEWIN' MY EAR CLEAN OFF, AS HE WAS WORKIN' ON DOIN' ALL EVENIN' (BOY BUT THAT WOLF COULD TALK!), AND GAVE ME TIME TA THINK.
DID I REALLY HEAR IT? 'LITTLEPIG?' COULD IT BE?
NAH, PROBABLY AS COMMON A NAME AMONG 'EM AS 'WOLF' IS AMONG OUR FOLK.
BUT WHAT IF...?
WHAT IF IT WERE TRUE? WHAT IF HE WERE RELATED TO...TO...
I HAD DECIDED TA GO THEN. RIGHT THEN AN' THERE I KNEW I HAD TA LEAVE.
THEY WAS LOOKIN' FO' ME AN' I WAS TOO CLOSE. DO THIS ONE JOB,
GET SOME CASH TA RIDE WITH, AN' I WAS GONE.
JUST ONE SMALL...

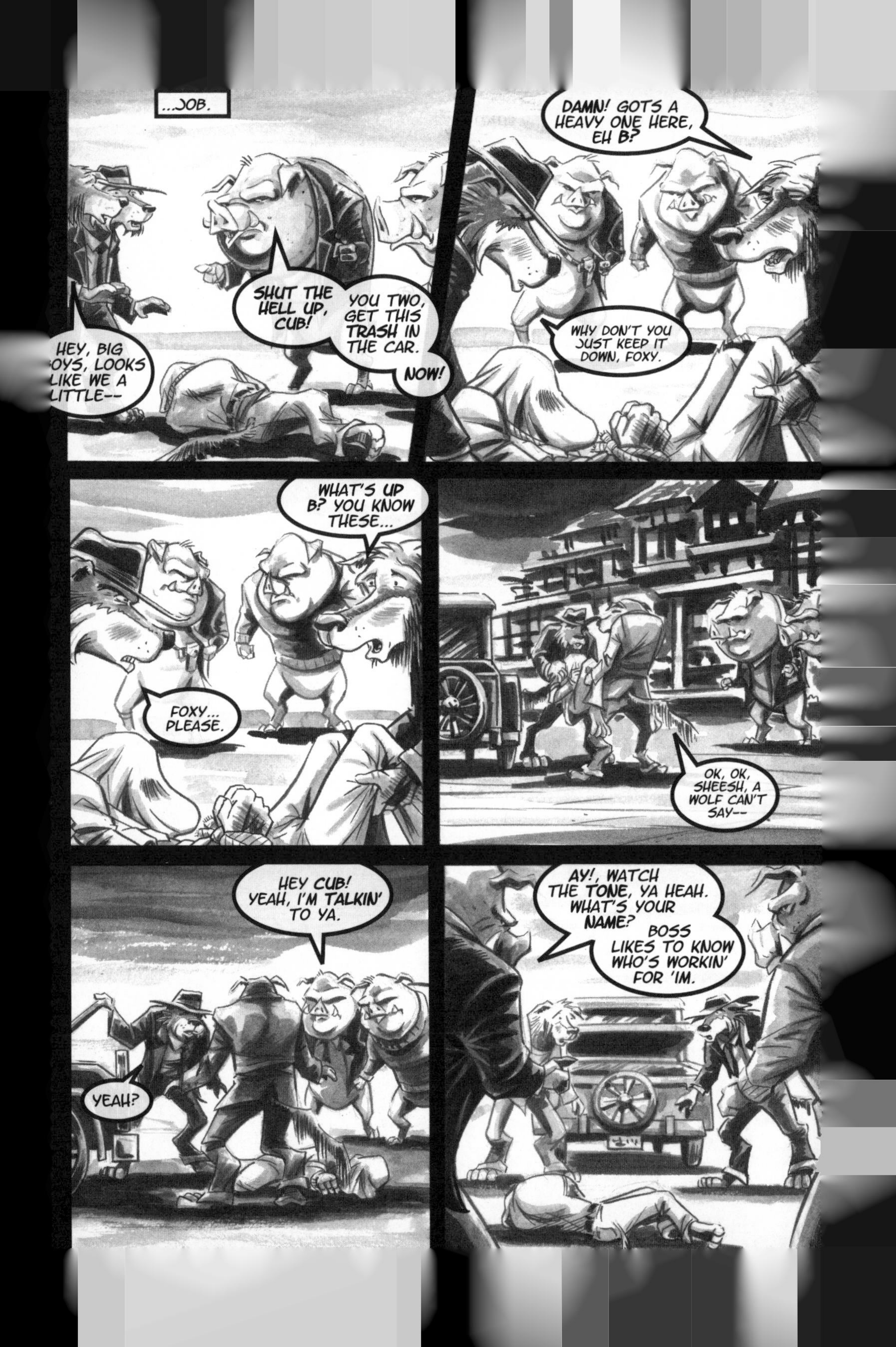
...JOB.
HEY, BIG BOYS, LOOKS LIKE WE A LITTLE--
SHUT THE HELL UP, CUB!
YOU TWO, GET THIS TRASH IN THE CAR.
NOW!
DAMN! GOTS A HEAVY ONE HERE, EH B?
WHY DON'T YOU JUST KEEP IT DOWN, FOXY.
WHAT'S UP B? YOU KNOW THESE...
FOXY... PLEASE.
OK, OK, SHEESH, A WOLF CAN'T SAY--
HEY CUB! YEAH, I'M TALKIN' TO YA.
YEAH?
AY!, WATCH THE TONE, YA HEAH. WHAT'S YOUR NAME?
BOSS LIKES TO KNOW WHO'S WORKIN' FOR 'IM.

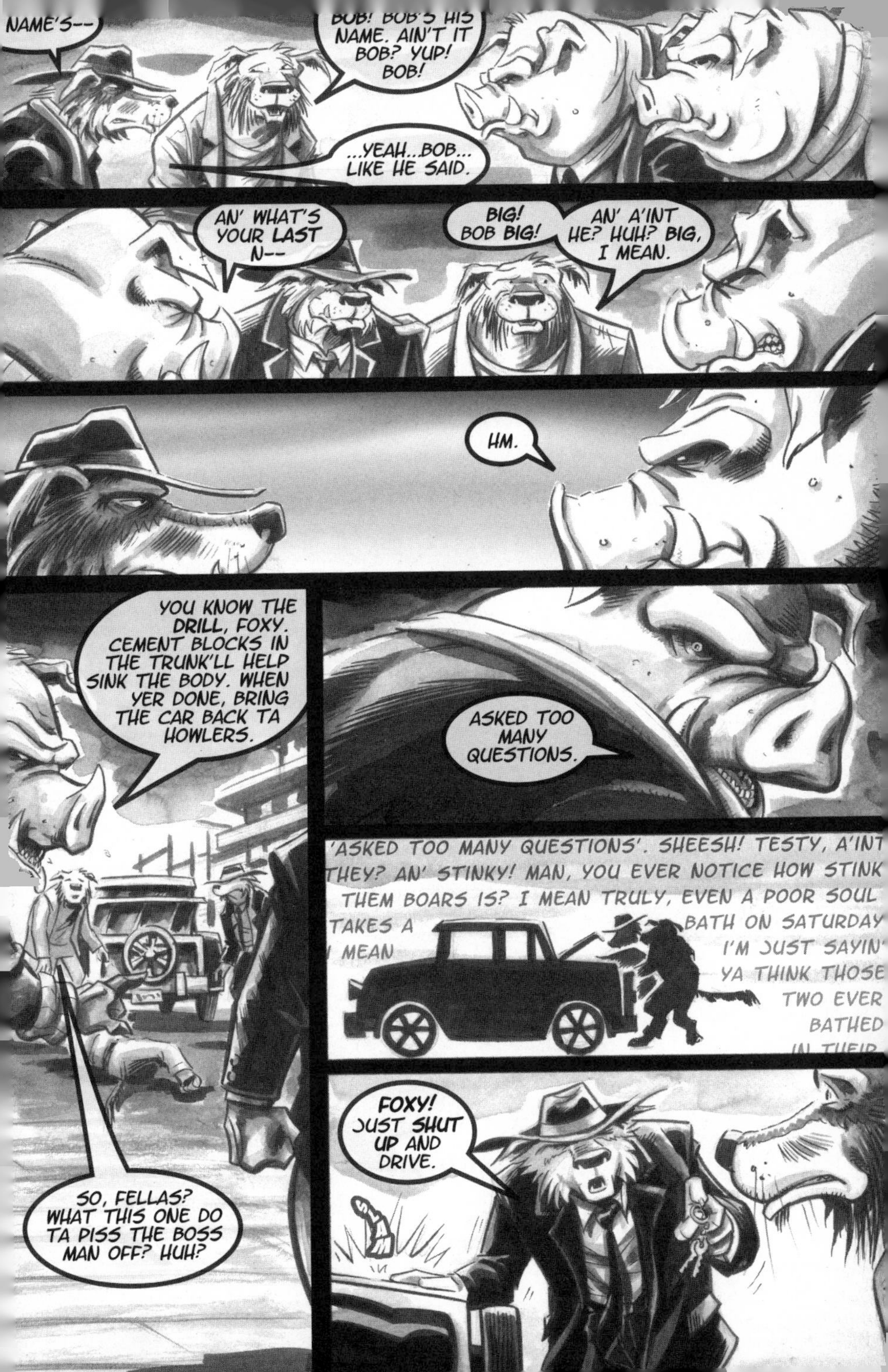
NAME'S--
BOB! BOB'S HIS NAME. AIN'T IT BOB? YUP! BOB!
...YEAH...BOB... LIKE HE SAID.
AN' WHAT'S YOUR LAST N--
BIG! BOB BIG!
AN' A'INT HE? HUH? BIG, I MEAN.
HM.
YOU KNOW THE DRILL, FOXY. CEMENT BLOCKS IN THE TRUNK'LL HELP SINK THE BODY. WHEN YER DONE, BRING THE CAR BACK TA HOWLERS.
SO, FELLAS? WHAT THIS ONE DO TA PISS THE BOSS MAN OFF? HUH?
ASKED TOO MANY QUESTIONS.
'ASKED TOO MANY QUESTIONS'. SHEESH! TESTY, A'INT THEY? AN' STINKY! MAN, YOU EVER NOTICE HOW STINK THEM BOARS IS? I MEAN TRULY, EVEN A POOR SOUL TAKES A BATH ON SATURDAY
MEAN I'M JUST SAYIN' YA THINK THOSE TWO EVER BATHED
FOXY! JUST SHUT UP AND DRIVE.

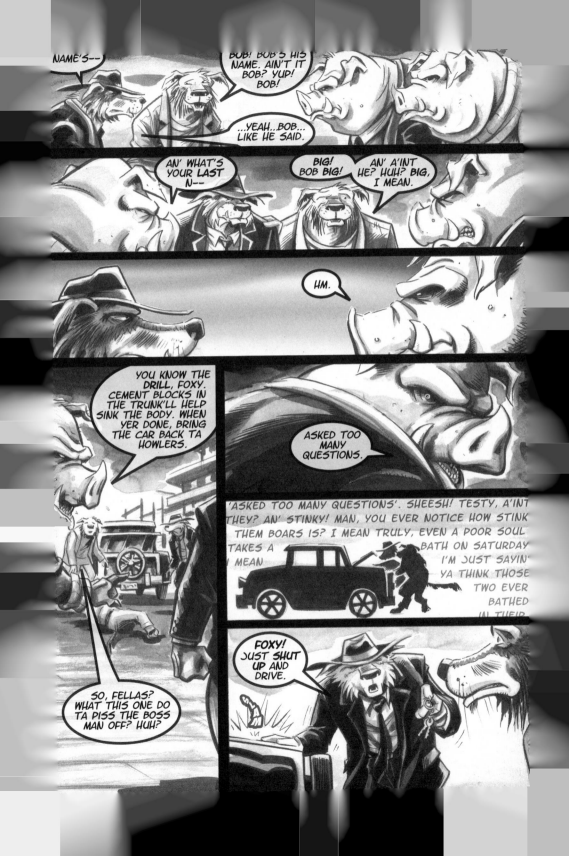

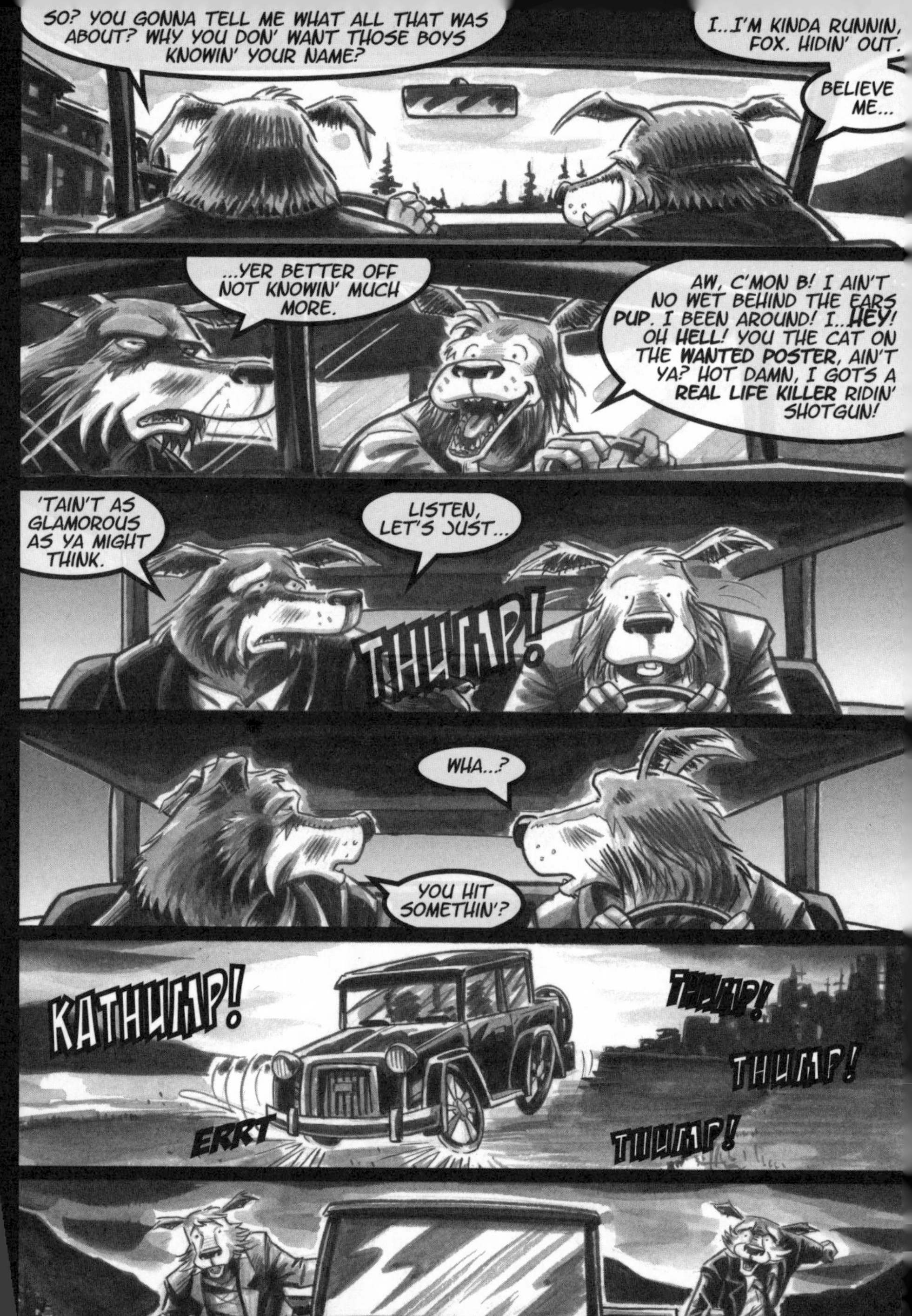
SO? YOU GONNA TELL ME WHAT ALL THAT WAS ABOUT? WHY YOU DON' WANT THOSE BOYS KNOWIN' YOUR NAME?
I..I'M KINDA RUNNIN, FOX. HIDIN' OUT.
BELIEVE ME...
...YER BETTER OFF NOT KNOWIN' MUCH MORE.
AW, C'MON B! I AIN'T NO WET BEHIND THE EARS PUP. I BEEN AROUND! I..HEY! OH HELL! YOU THE CAT ON THE WANTED POSTER, AIN'T YA? HOT DAMN, I GOTS A REAL LIFE KILLER RIDIN' SHOTGUN!
'TAIN'T AS GLAMOROUS AS YA MIGHT THINK.
LISTEN, LET'S JUST...
THUMP!
WHA..?
YOU HIT SOMETHIN'?
KATHUMP!
THUMP!
THUMP!
ERRT
THUMP!

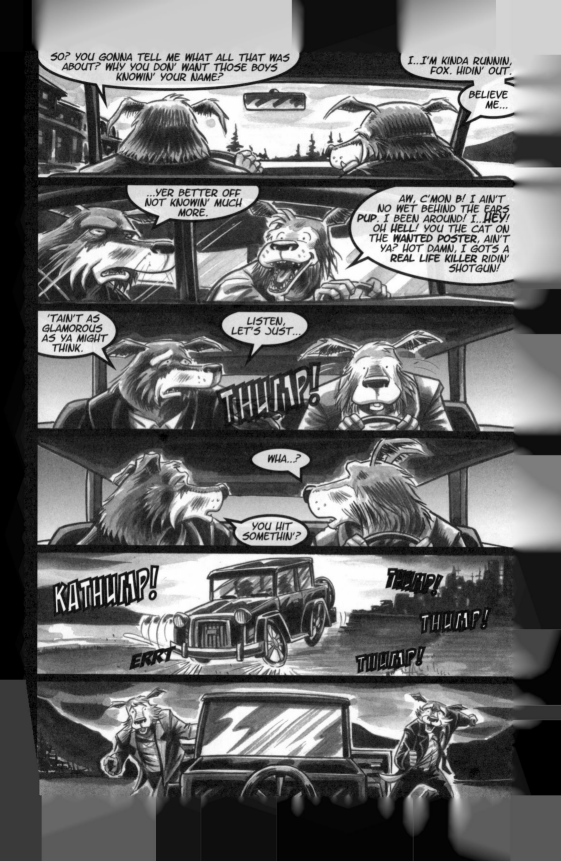

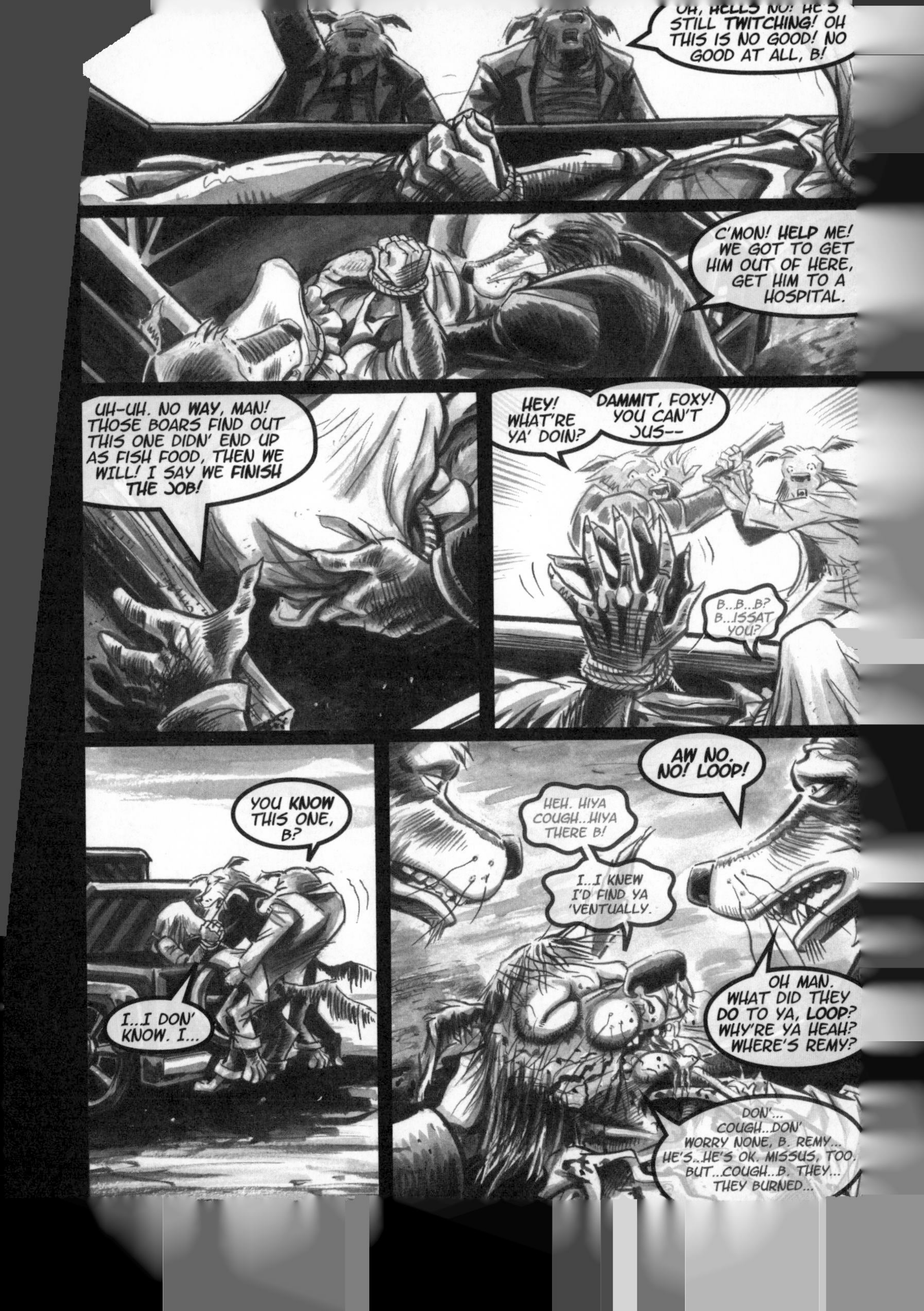
OH, HELLS NO! HE'S STILL TWITCHING! OH THIS IS NO GOOD! NO GOOD AT ALL, B!
C'MON! HELP ME! WE GOT TO GET HIM OUT OF HERE, GET HIM TO A HOSPITAL.
UH-UH. NO WAY, MAN! THOSE BOARS FIND OUT THIS ONE DIDN' END UP AS FISH FOOD, THEN WE WILL! I SAY WE FINISH THE JOB!
HEY! WHAT'RE YA' DOIN?
DAMMIT, FOXY! YOU CAN'T JUS--
B...B...B? B...ISSAT YOU?
YOU KNOW THIS ONE, B?
I...I DON' KNOW. I...
AW NO. NO! LOOP!
HEH. HIYA COUGH...HIYA THERE B!
I...I KNEW I'D FIND YA 'VENTUALLY.
OH MAN. WHAT DID THEY DO TO YA, LOOP? WHY'RE YA HEAH? WHERE'S REMY?
DON'... COUGH...DON' WORRY NONE, B. REMY... HE'S...HE'S OK. MISSUS, TOO. BUT...COUGH...B. THEY... THEY BURNED...

THOUGH IT TOOK HIM A SPELL,
TALKIN' THROUGH BROKEN TEETH
AND BLOOD, LOOP TOL' ME WHAT
HAPPENED AFTER I LEFT MONEY.
SEEMS AFTER I SLAUGHTERED MR.
LITTLEPIG, ALL HELL BROKE
LOOSE.

WE'D SEEN THE PINK HOODS
BEFORE, O' COURSE. WE ALL KNEW IT
WAS THEM THAT...THAT... BUT NOW WE
HAD FACES UNDER THE HOODS.
THE LITTLEPIGS.

TURNS OUT THE
FIRST LITTLEPIG
HAD TWO BROTHERS,
AN' THEY WAS NONE
TOO HAPPY 'BOUT
WHAT I'D DONE TO
THE LITTLEST ONE.
SO, THEY HIT BACK
AGAIN. WEREN'T
JUST LOOP'S FARM,
NEITHER. NO,
THEY WENT ON
A REAL 'SCORCHED
EARTH' TOUR.
BURNED EVERYTHIN'
IN THEIR PATH,
ACCORDIN'
TA LOOP.

WOULDA' HAPPENED
ANYWAY, LOOP SAID.
ONLY A MATTER
OF TIME.

SEE, THE ELDEST PIG, BIG SHOT INDUSTRIALIST UP IN CHI TOWN, HE HAD THIS
PLAN. CONTROL OF THE WHOLE MISSISSIPPI RIVER VALLEY. HE ALREADY OWNED ENOUGH
LAND, INDUSTRY AND JUST ABOUT ALL THE SHIPPING LINES COMING OUT OF THE LAKES
TA BE CONSIDERED TOP PIG IN THE NORTH.

SECOND LITTLEPIG, LOOP
SAID, WAS RIGHT HEAH IN E. ST. LOUIS.
ALREADY A BIG SHOT CLUB OWNER AND
CONTROLLING ALL THE 'DARK'
INDUSTRY. GAMBLIN', HOOKERS, RUM.
HELL, WEREN'T NUTHIN' WORTH ANYTHIN'
THAT HE DIDN' HAVE A HAND IN. COURSE,
ALL THAT CAME IN THROUGH THE
DOCKS LIKE EVERYTHIN' ELSE. SO
NATURALLY, HE OWNED
THE DOCKS TOO.

AND THEN THERE'S
LITTLEPIG NUMBER THREE, THE ONE
WHOSE BLOOD IS STILL STUCK IN
MY NAILS. WITH THE HELP OF BIG
LITTLEPIG HE WAS BUYIN' EVERY PIECE
OF LAND HE COULD GET HIS GRUBBY
LITTLE HOOVES ON.

OFFERED US MORE
MONEY THAN MOST OF US
HAD EVER SEEN AN' IT WAS STILL
LESS THAN A TENTH A' WHAT THE
FARMS WAS REALLY WORTH.

AN' THOSE
THAT REFUSED
TA SELL?...

WELL...

BUT THAT'S WHERE THEY MESSED UP, SEE?
THEY REALLY THOUGHT WE WEREN'T A THREAT.
THEY TRULY BELIEVE IN ALL THAT
'SUPERIOR RACE' CRAP. THEY THOUGHT
THEY WAS FREAKIN' BLESSED, ON A
'HOLY CRUSADE'. ARROGANT BASTARDS!

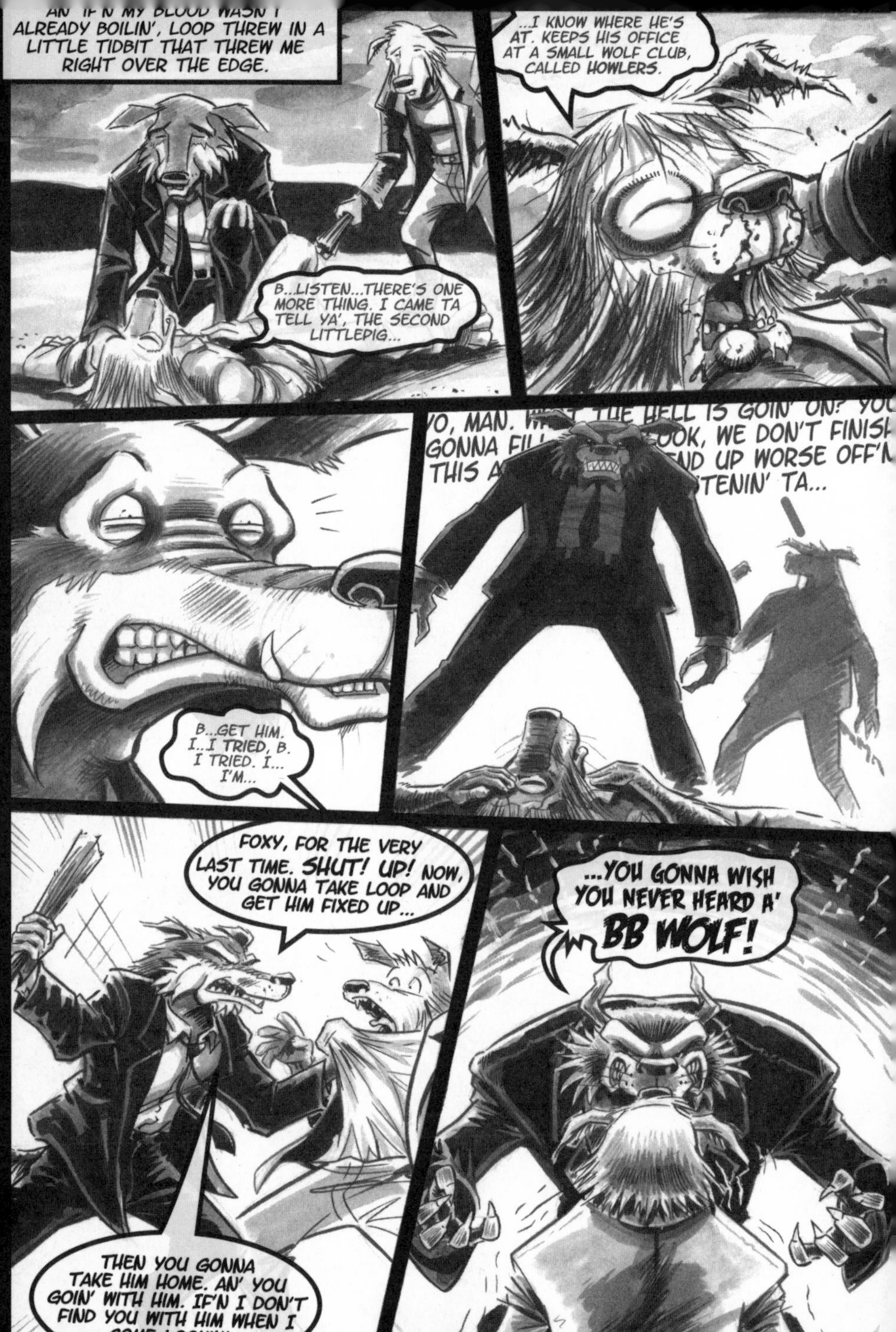
AN' IF'N MY BLOOD WASN'T ALREADY BOILIN', LOOP THREW IN A LITTLE TIDBIT THAT THREW ME RIGHT OVER THE EDGE.
...I KNOW WHERE HE'S AT. KEEPS HIS OFFICE AT A SMALL WOLF CLUB, CALLED HOWLERS.
B...LISTEN...THERE'S ONE MORE THING. I CAME TA TELL YA', THE SECOND LITTLEPIG...
B...GET HIM. I..I TRIED, B. I TRIED. I... I'M...
YO, MAN.
THE HELL IS GOIN' ON?
GONNA FI
OOK, WE DON'T FINISH
THIS A
END UP WORSE OFF'N
STENIN' TA...
FOXY, FOR THE VERY LAST TIME. SHUT! UP! NOW, YOU GONNA TAKE LOOP AND GET HIM FIXED UP...
THEN YOU GONNA TAKE HIM HOME. AN' YOU GOIN' WITH HIM. IF'N I DON'T FIND YOU WITH HIM WHEN I COME LOOKIN'...
...YOU GONNA WISH YOU NEVER HEARD A' BB WOLF!

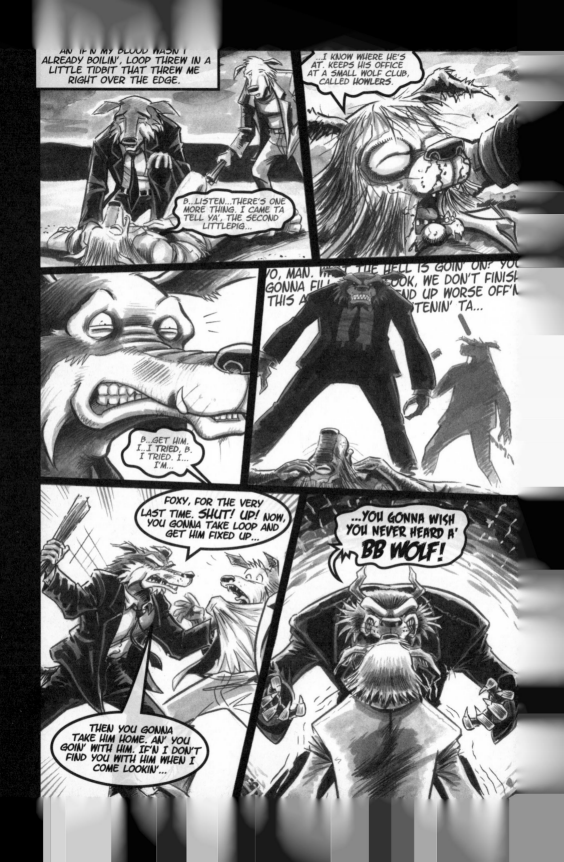

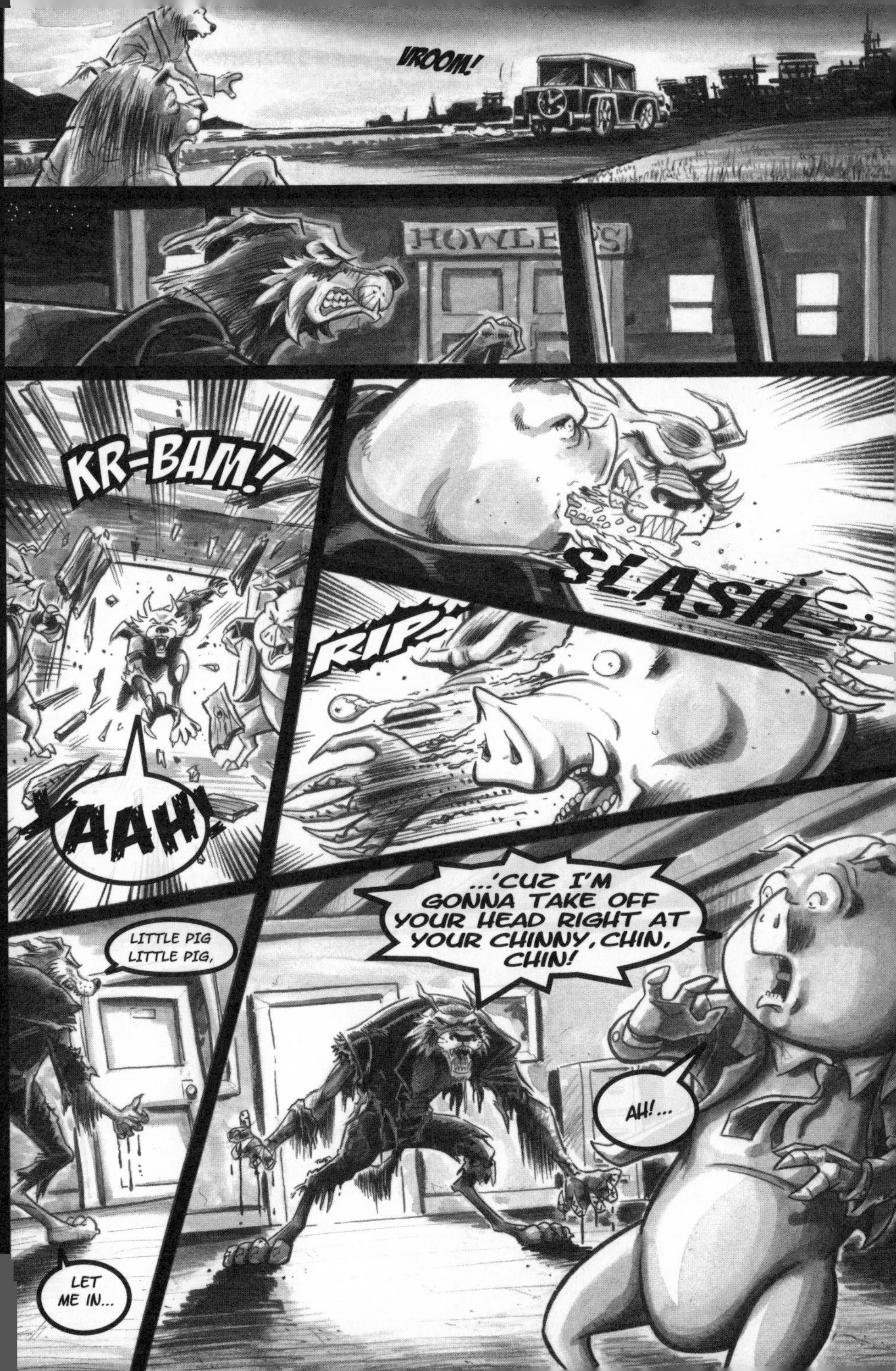
VROOM!
HOWLER'S
KR-BAM!
SLASH
RIP
AAH
LITTLE PIG
LITTLE PIG,
LET
ME IN...
...'CUZ I'M GONNA TAKE OFF YOUR HEAD RIGHT AT YOUR CHINNY, CHIN, CHIN!
AH!...

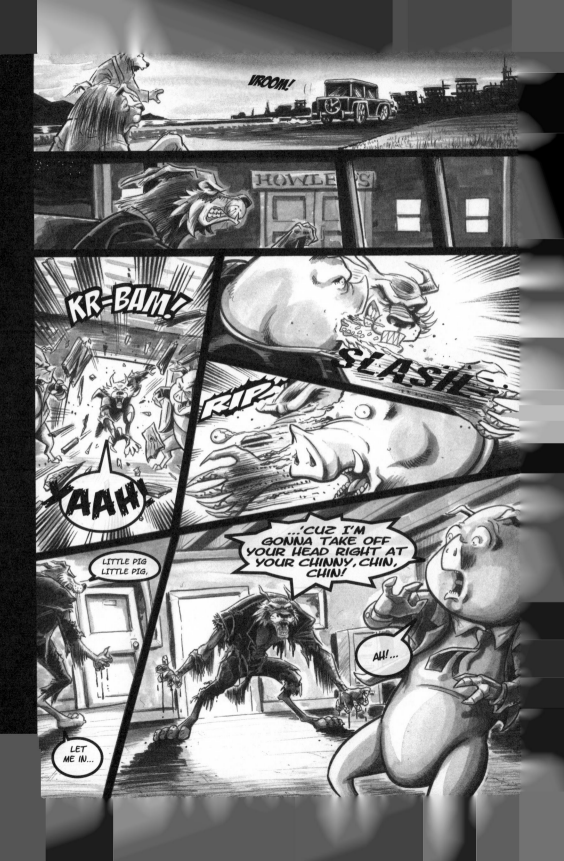

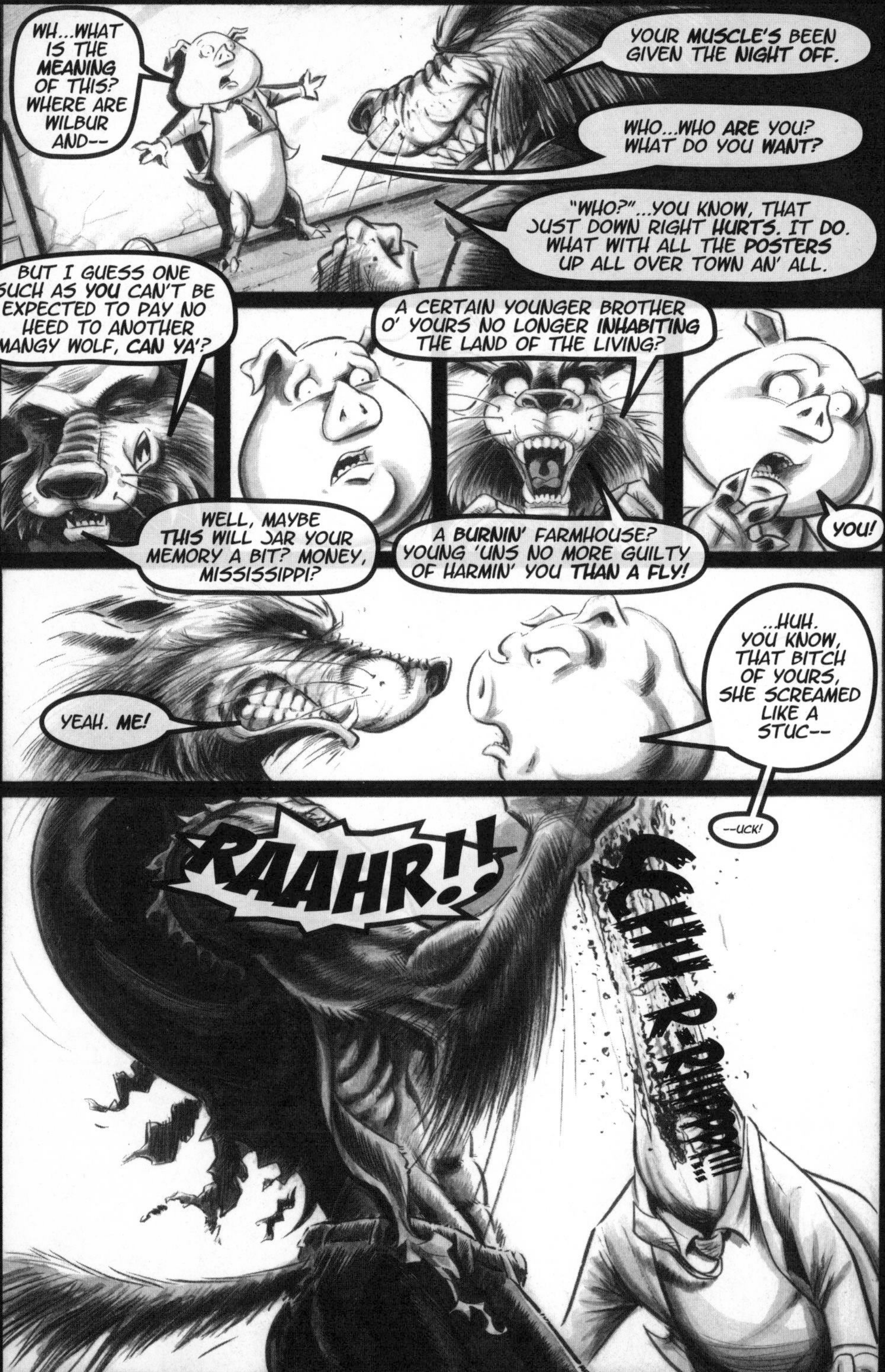
WH...WHAT IS THE MEANING OF THIS? WHERE ARE WILBUR AND--
YOUR MUSCLE'S BEEN GIVEN THE NIGHT OFF.
WHO...WHO ARE YOU? WHAT DO YOU WANT?
"WHO?"...YOU KNOW, THAT JUST DOWN RIGHT HURTS. IT DO. WHAT WITH ALL THE POSTERS UP ALL OVER TOWN AN' ALL.
BUT I GUESS ONE SUCH AS YOU CAN'T BE EXPECTED TO PAY NO HEED TO ANOTHER MANGY WOLF, CAN YA'?
WELL, MAYBE THIS WILL JAR YOUR MEMORY A BIT? MONEY, MISSISSIPPI?
A CERTAIN YOUNGER BROTHER O' YOURS NO LONGER INHABITING THE LAND OF THE LIVING?
A BURNIN' FARMHOUSE? YOUNG 'UNS NO MORE GUILTY OF HARMIN' YOU THAN A FLY!
YOU!
YEAH. ME!
...HUH. YOU KNOW, THAT BITCH OF YOURS, SHE SCREAMED LIKE A STUC--
--UCK!
RAAHR!!
SCHHH-R-RIPPP!!!

Sure enough to knock a man to his knees.
—The Commodores, *Brick House*

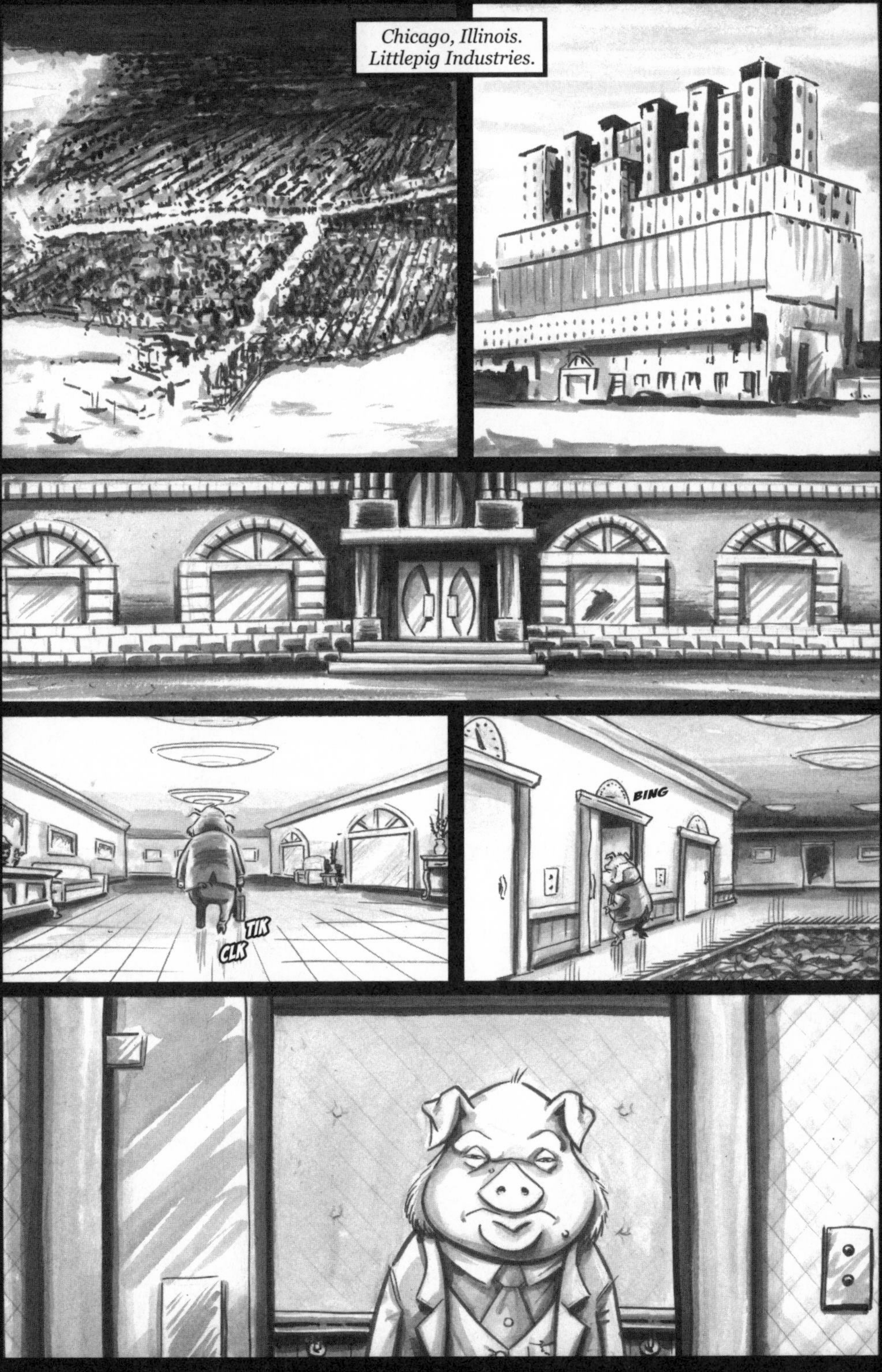

Chicago, Illinois.
Littlepig Industries.
TIK
CLK
BING

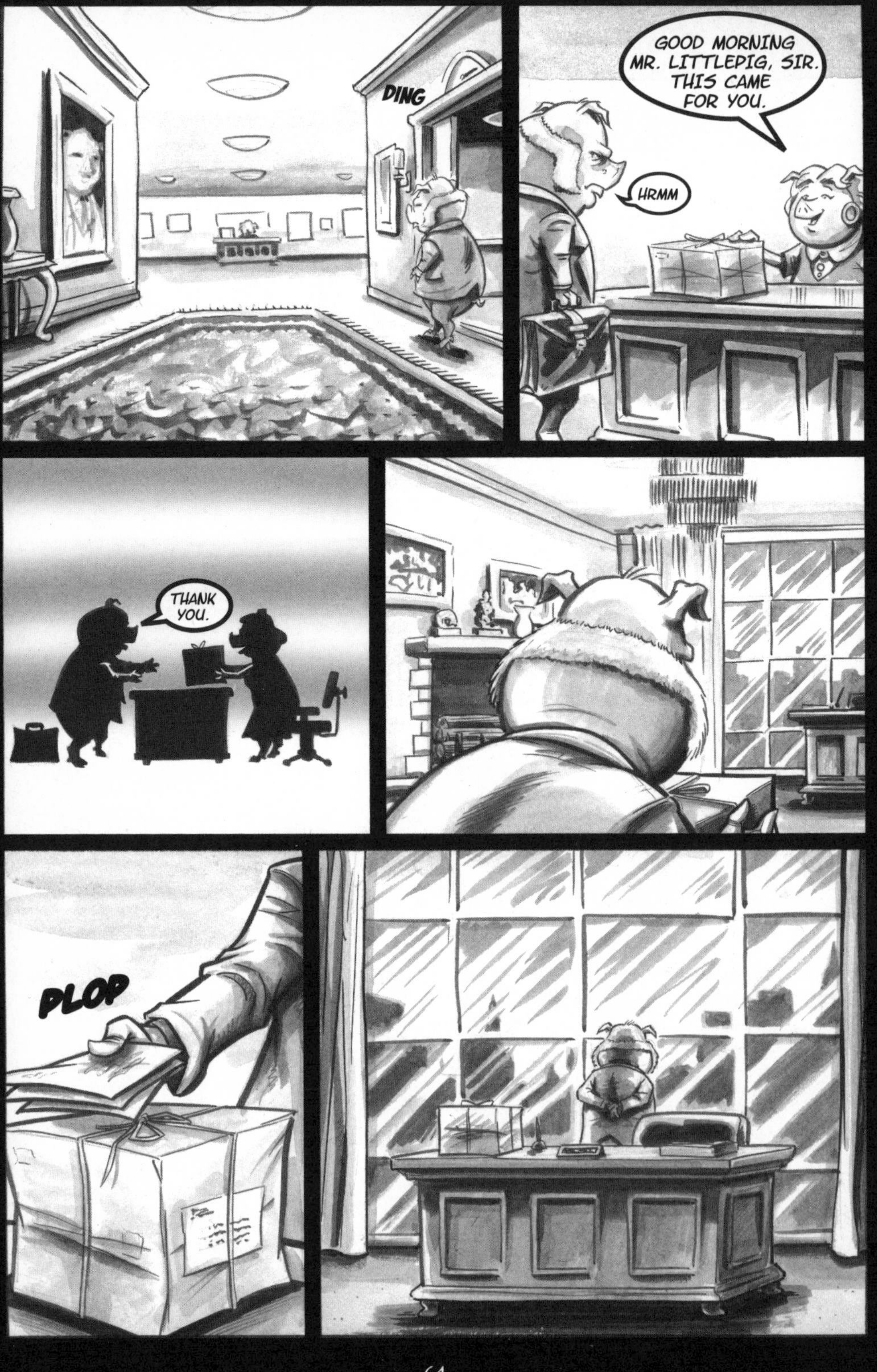
DING
GOOD MORNING MR. LITTLEPIG, SIR. THIS CAME FOR YOU.
HRMM
THANK YOU.
PLOP

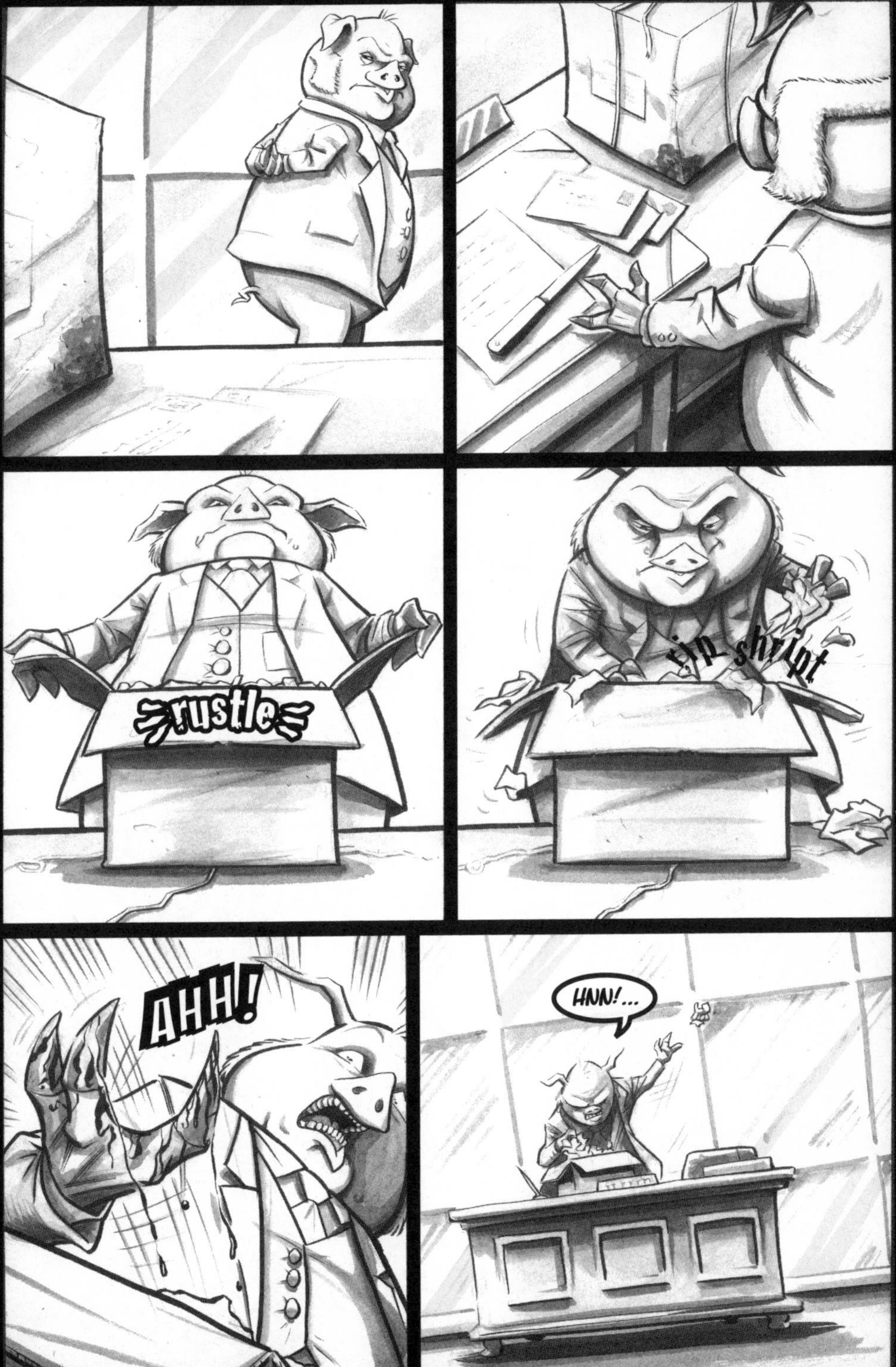
rustle
rip shript
AHH!
HNN!...

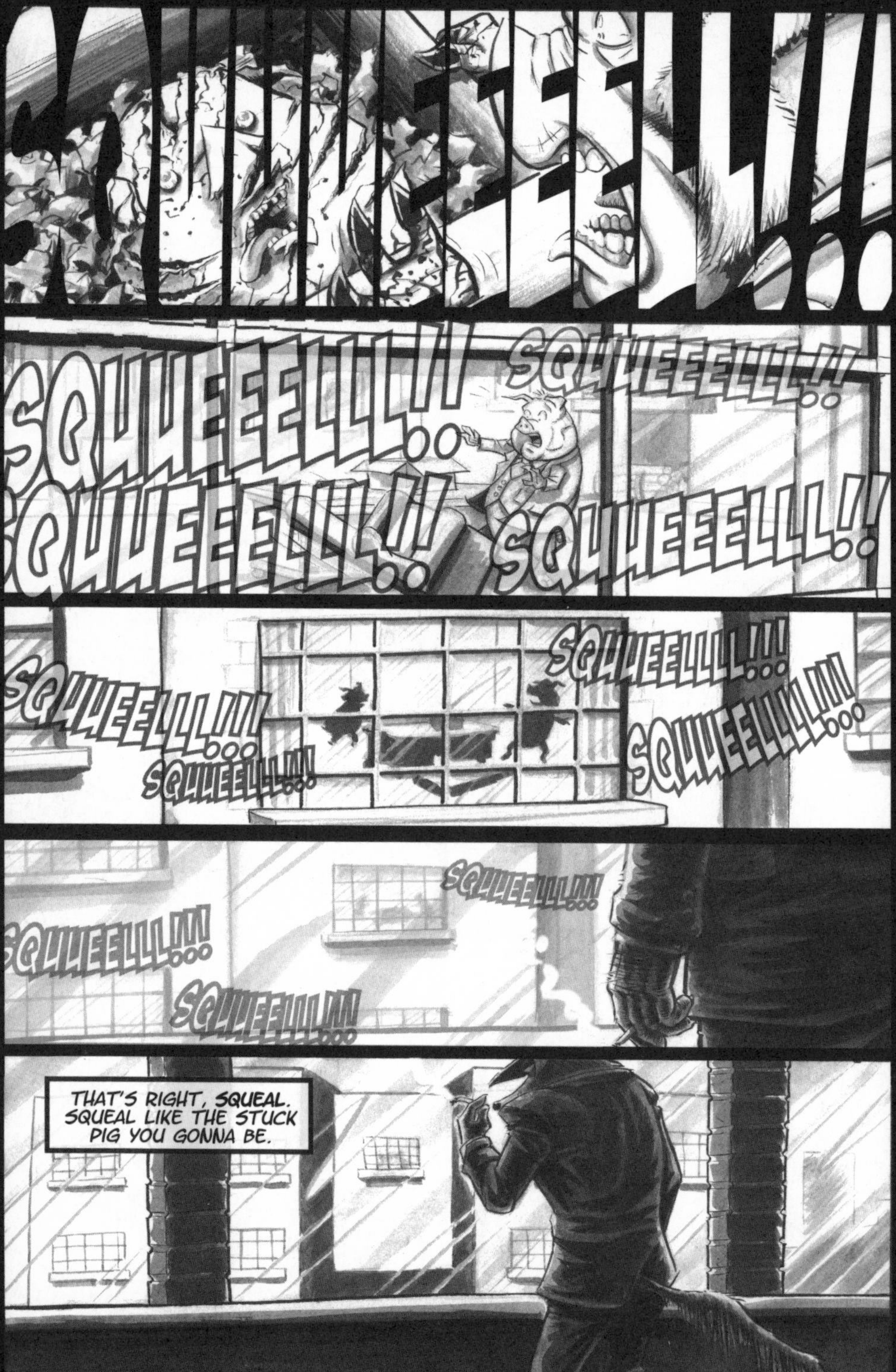
SQUEEELLL!!..
SQUUEEEELLL!!..
SQUEEELLL!!..
SQUUEEEELLL!!..
SQUEELLL!!!...
SQUEELLL!!!...
SQUEELLL!!!...
SQUEELLLL!!!...
SQUEELLL!!!...
SQUEELLL!!!...
SQUEELLL!!!...
THAT'S RIGHT, SQUEAL. SQUEAL LIKE THE STUCK PIG YOU GONNA BE.

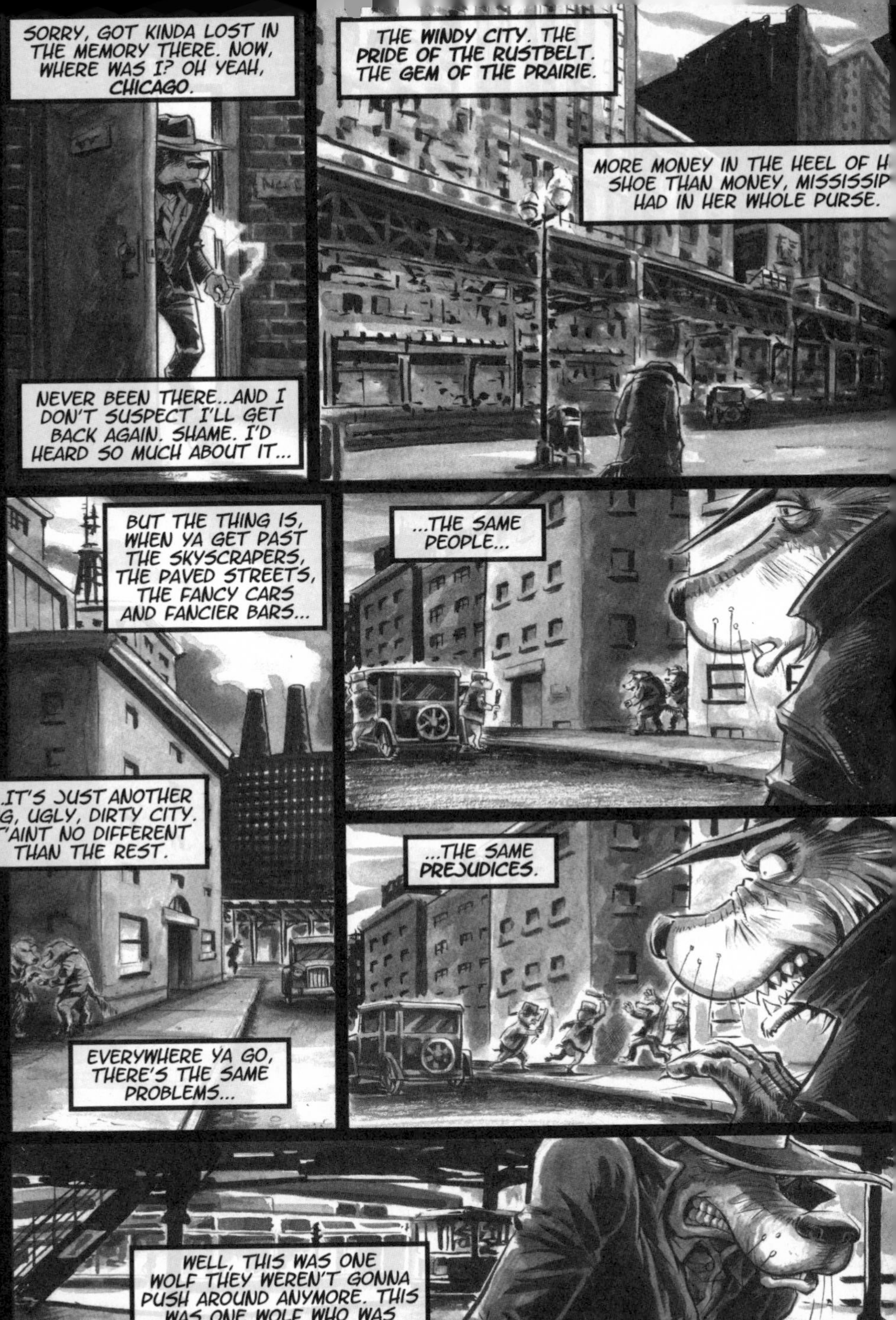
SORRY, GOT KINDA LOST IN THE MEMORY THERE. NOW, WHERE WAS I? OH YEAH, CHICAGO.
NEVER BEEN THERE...AND I DON'T SUSPECT I'LL GET BACK AGAIN. SHAME. I'D HEARD SO MUCH ABOUT IT...
THE WINDY CITY. THE PRIDE OF THE RUSTBELT. THE GEM OF THE PRAIRIE.
MORE MONEY IN THE HEEL OF H SHOE THAN MONEY, MISSISSIP HAD IN HER WHOLE PURSE.
BUT THE THING IS, WHEN YA GET PAST THE SKYSCRAPERS, THE PAVED STREETS, THE FANCY CARS AND FANCIER BARS...
...IT'S JUST ANOTHER BIG, UGLY, DIRTY CITY. T'AINT NO DIFFERENT THAN THE REST.
EVERYWHERE YA GO, THERE'S THE SAME PROBLEMS...
...THE SAME PEOPLE...
...THE SAME PREJUDICES.
WELL, THIS WAS ONE WOLF THEY WEREN'T GONNA PUSH AROUND ANYMORE. THIS WAS ONE WOLF WHO WAS MAKIN' A STAND. EVEN IF IT KILLED HIM.

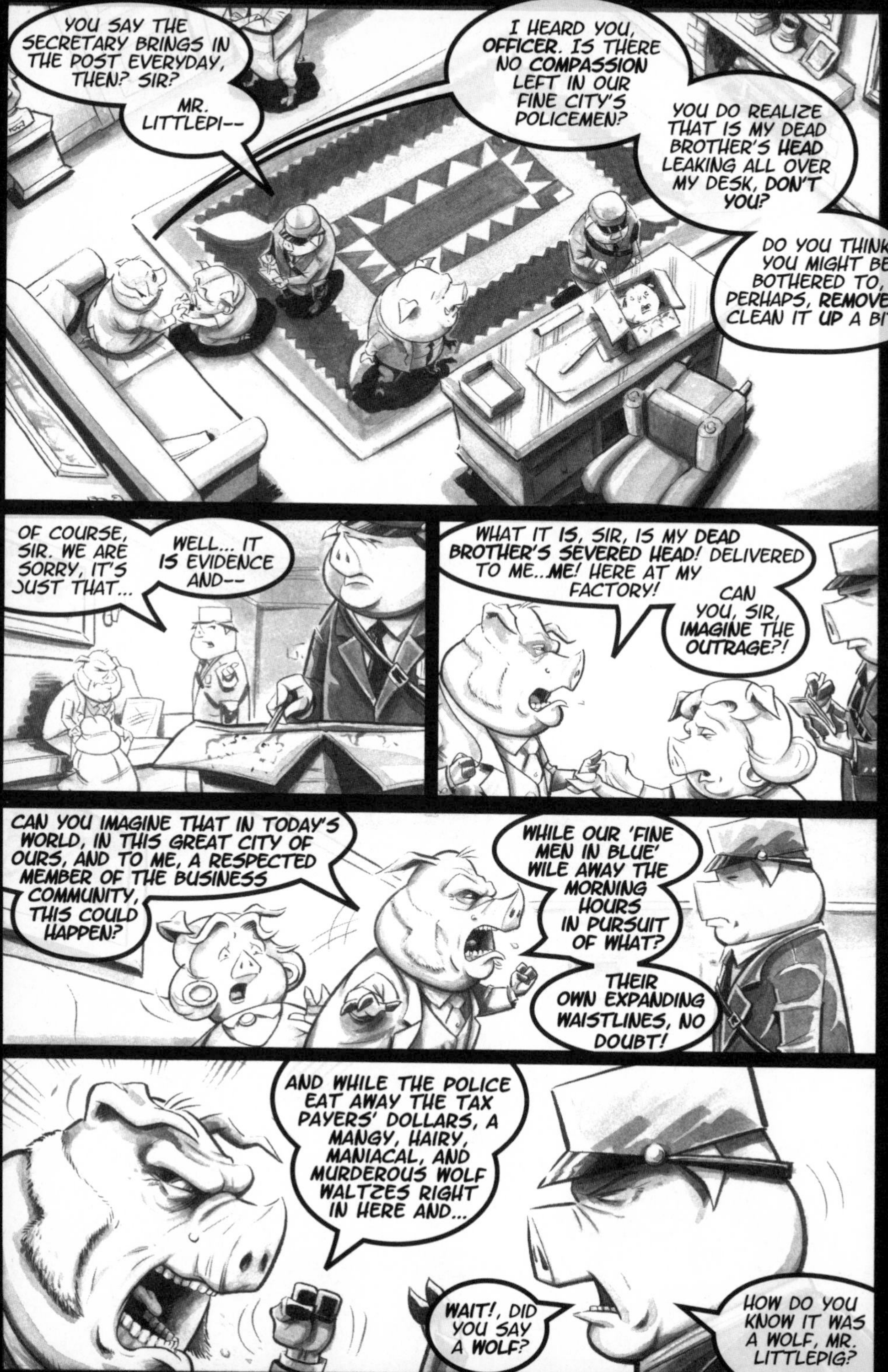
YOU SAY THE SECRETARY BRINGS IN THE POST EVERYDAY, THEN? SIR?
MR. LITTLEPI--
I HEARD YOU, OFFICER. IS THERE NO COMPASSION LEFT IN OUR FINE CITY'S POLICEMEN?
YOU DO REALIZE THAT IS MY DEAD BROTHER'S HEAD LEAKING ALL OVER MY DESK, DON'T YOU?
DO YOU THINK YOU MIGHT BE BOTHERED TO, PERHAPS, REMOVE IT? CLEAN IT UP A BIT?
OF COURSE, SIR. WE ARE SORRY, IT'S JUST THAT...
WELL... IT IS EVIDENCE AND--
WHAT IT IS, SIR, IS MY DEAD BROTHER'S SEVERED HEAD! DELIVERED TO ME...ME! HERE AT MY FACTORY!
CAN YOU, SIR, IMAGINE THE OUTRAGE?!
CAN YOU IMAGINE THAT IN TODAY'S WORLD, IN THIS GREAT CITY OF OURS, AND TO ME, A RESPECTED MEMBER OF THE BUSINESS COMMUNITY, THIS COULD HAPPEN?
WHILE OUR 'FINE MEN IN BLUE' WILE AWAY THE MORNING HOURS IN PURSUIT OF WHAT?
THEIR OWN EXPANDING WAISTLINES, NO DOUBT!
AND WHILE THE POLICE EAT AWAY THE TAX PAYERS' DOLLARS, A MANGY, HAIRY, MANIACAL, AND MURDEROUS WOLF WALTZES RIGHT IN HERE AND...
WAIT!, DID YOU SAY A WOLF?
HOW DO YOU KNOW IT WAS A WOLF, MR. LITTLEPIG?

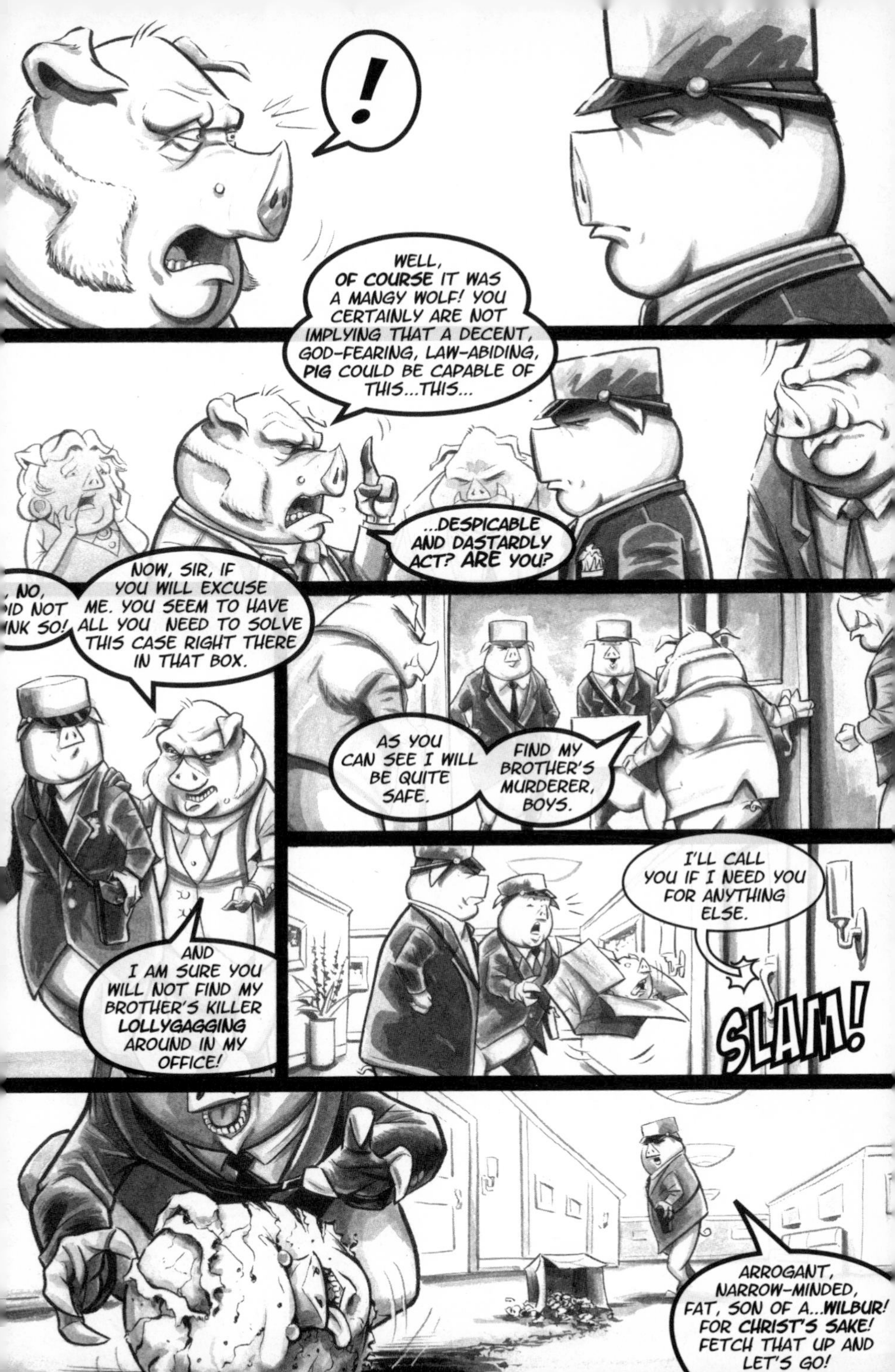
!
WELL, OF COURSE IT WAS A MANGY WOLF! YOU CERTAINLY ARE NOT IMPLYING THAT A DECENT, GOD-FEARING, LAW-ABIDING, PIG COULD BE CAPABLE OF THIS...THIS...
...DESPICABLE AND DASTARDLY ACT? ARE YOU?
NOW, SIR, IF YOU WILL EXCUSE ME. YOU SEEM TO HAVE ALL YOU NEED TO SOLVE THIS CASE RIGHT THERE IN THAT BOX.
AND I AM SURE YOU WILL NOT FIND MY BROTHER'S KILLER LOLLYGAGGING AROUND IN MY OFFICE!
AS YOU CAN SEE I WILL BE QUITE SAFE.
FIND MY BROTHER'S MURDERER, BOYS.
I'LL CALL YOU IF I NEED YOU FOR ANYTHING ELSE.
SLAM!
ARROGANT, NARROW-MINDED, FAT, SON OF A...WILBUR! FOR CHRIST'S SAKE! FETCH THAT UP AND LET'S GO!

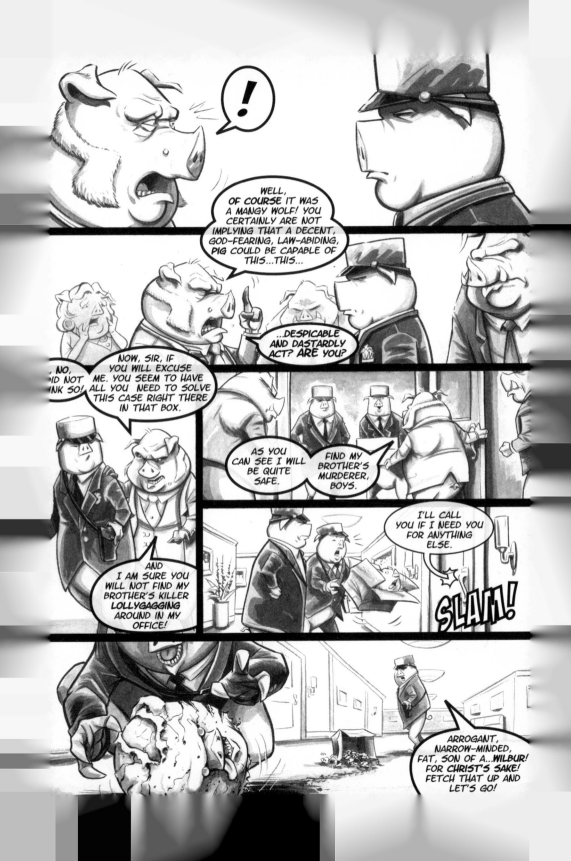

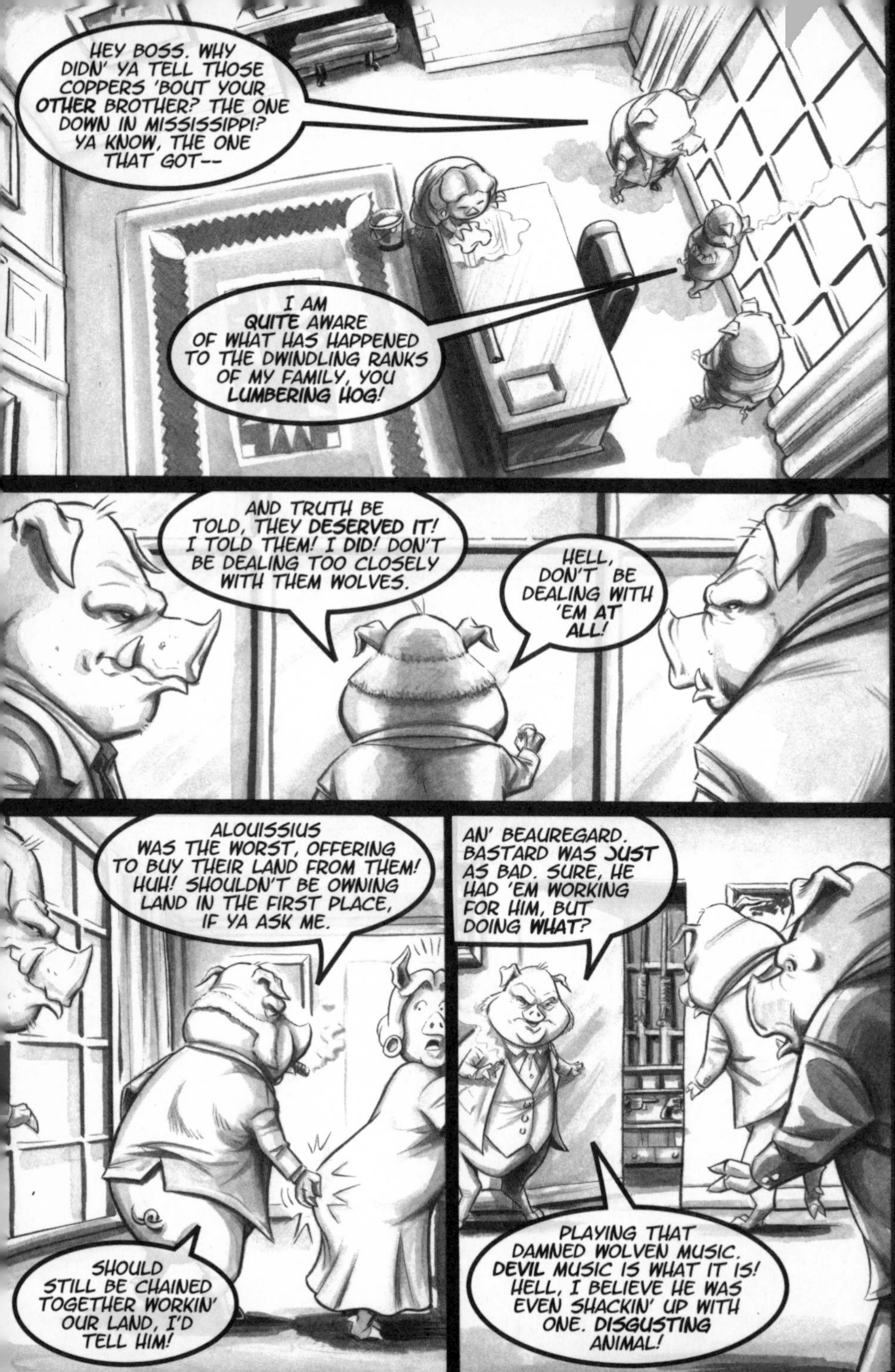
HEY BOSS. WHY DIDN' YA TELL THOSE COPPERS 'BOUT YOUR OTHER BROTHER? THE ONE DOWN IN MISSISSIPPI? YA KNOW, THE ONE THAT GOT--
I AM QUITE AWARE OF WHAT HAS HAPPENED TO THE DWINDLING RANKS OF MY FAMILY, YOU LUMBERING HOG!
AND TRUTH BE TOLD, THEY DESERVED IT! I TOLD THEM! I DID! DON'T BE DEALING TOO CLOSELY WITH THEM WOLVES.
HELL, DON'T BE DEALING WITH 'EM AT ALL!
ALOUISSIUS WAS THE WORST, OFFERING TO BUY THEIR LAND FROM THEM! HUH! SHOULDN'T BE OWNING LAND IN THE FIRST PLACE, IF YA ASK ME.
SHOULD STILL BE CHAINED TOGETHER WORKIN' OUR LAND, I'D TELL HIM!
AN' BEAUREGARD. BASTARD WAS JUST AS BAD. SURE, HE HAD 'EM WORKING FOR HIM, BUT DOING WHAT?
PLAYING THAT DAMNED WOLVEN MUSIC. DEVIL MUSIC IS WHAT IT IS! HELL, I BELIEVE HE WAS EVEN SHACKIN' UP WITH ONE. DISGUSTING ANIMAL!

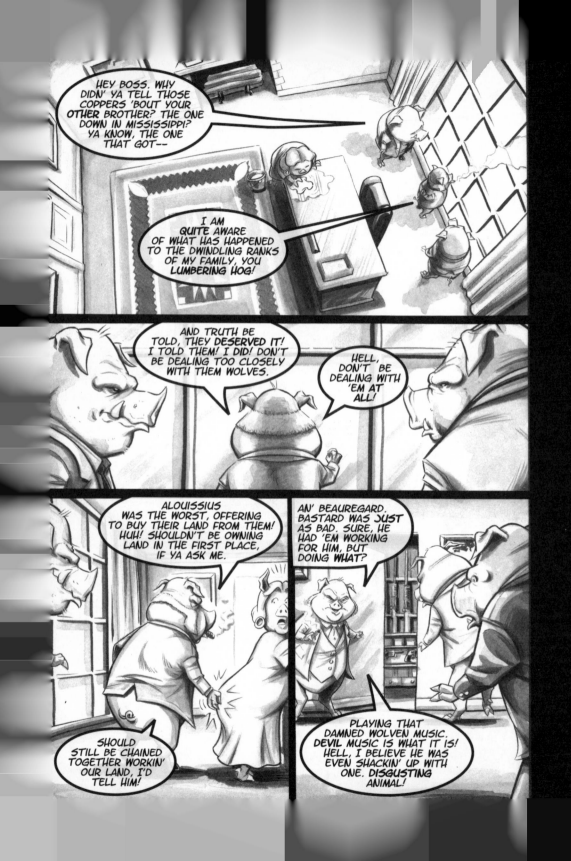

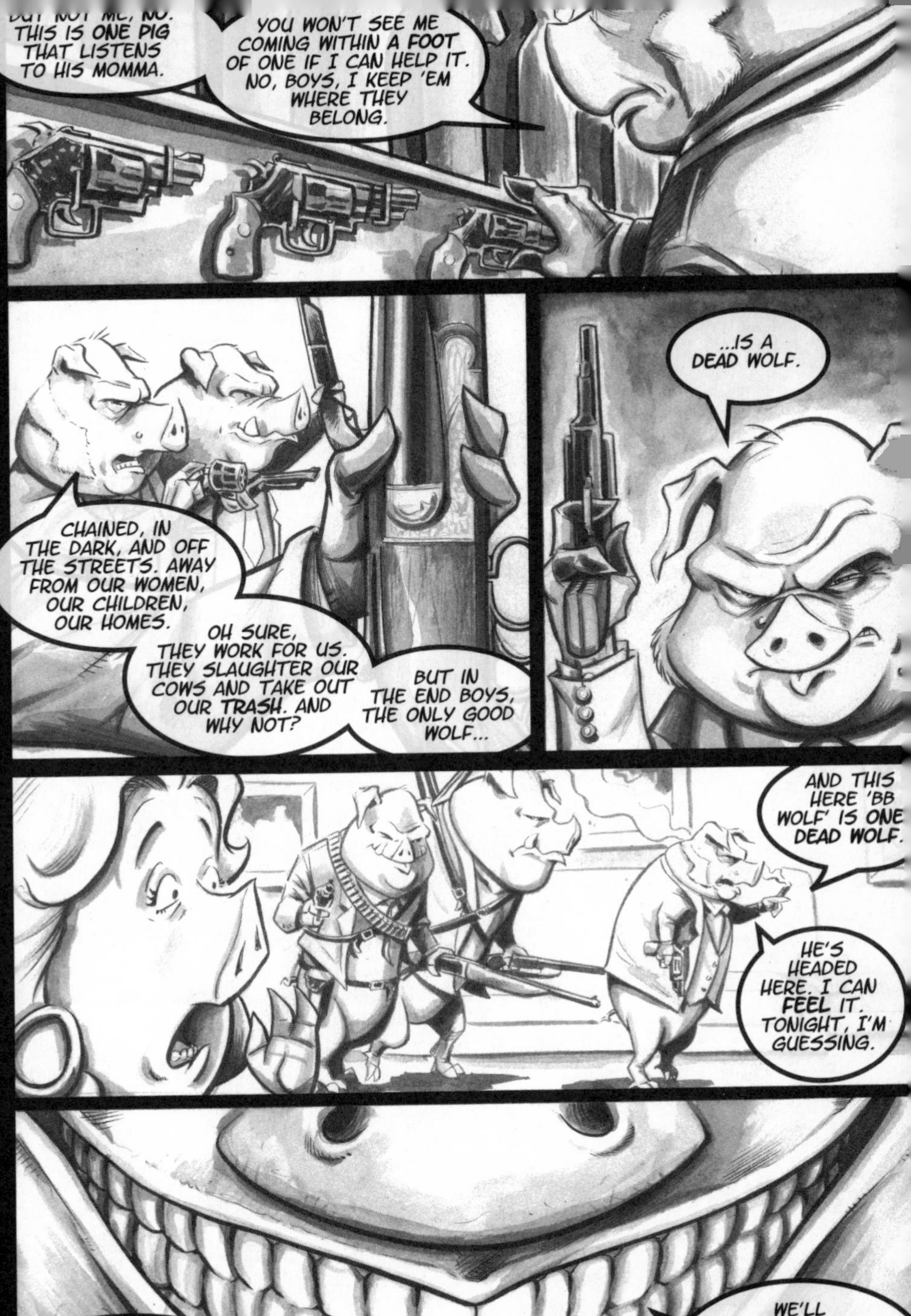
THIS IS ONE PIG THAT LISTENS TO HIS MOMMA.
YOU WON'T SEE ME COMING WITHIN A FOOT OF ONE IF I CAN HELP IT. NO, BOYS, I KEEP 'EM WHERE THEY BELONG.
CHAINED, IN THE DARK, AND OFF THE STREETS. AWAY FROM OUR WOMEN, OUR CHILDREN, OUR HOMES.
OH SURE, THEY WORK FOR US. THEY SLAUGHTER OUR COWS AND TAKE OUT OUR TRASH. AND WHY NOT?
BUT IN THE END BOYS, THE ONLY GOOD WOLF...
...IS A DEAD WOLF.
AND THIS HERE 'BB WOLF' IS ONE DEAD WOLF.
HE'S HEADED HERE. I CAN FEEL IT. TONIGHT, I'M GUESSING.
GO FETCH THE TROOPS, BOYS. WE'RE HAVING A SLEEP OVER.
WE'LL SHOW MR. WOLF HE HAS MESSED WITH THE WRONG DAMNED PIG!

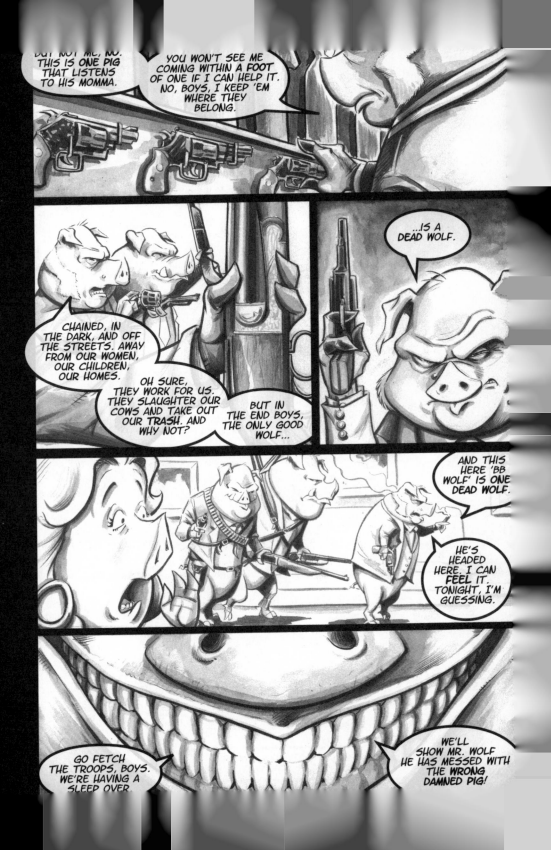

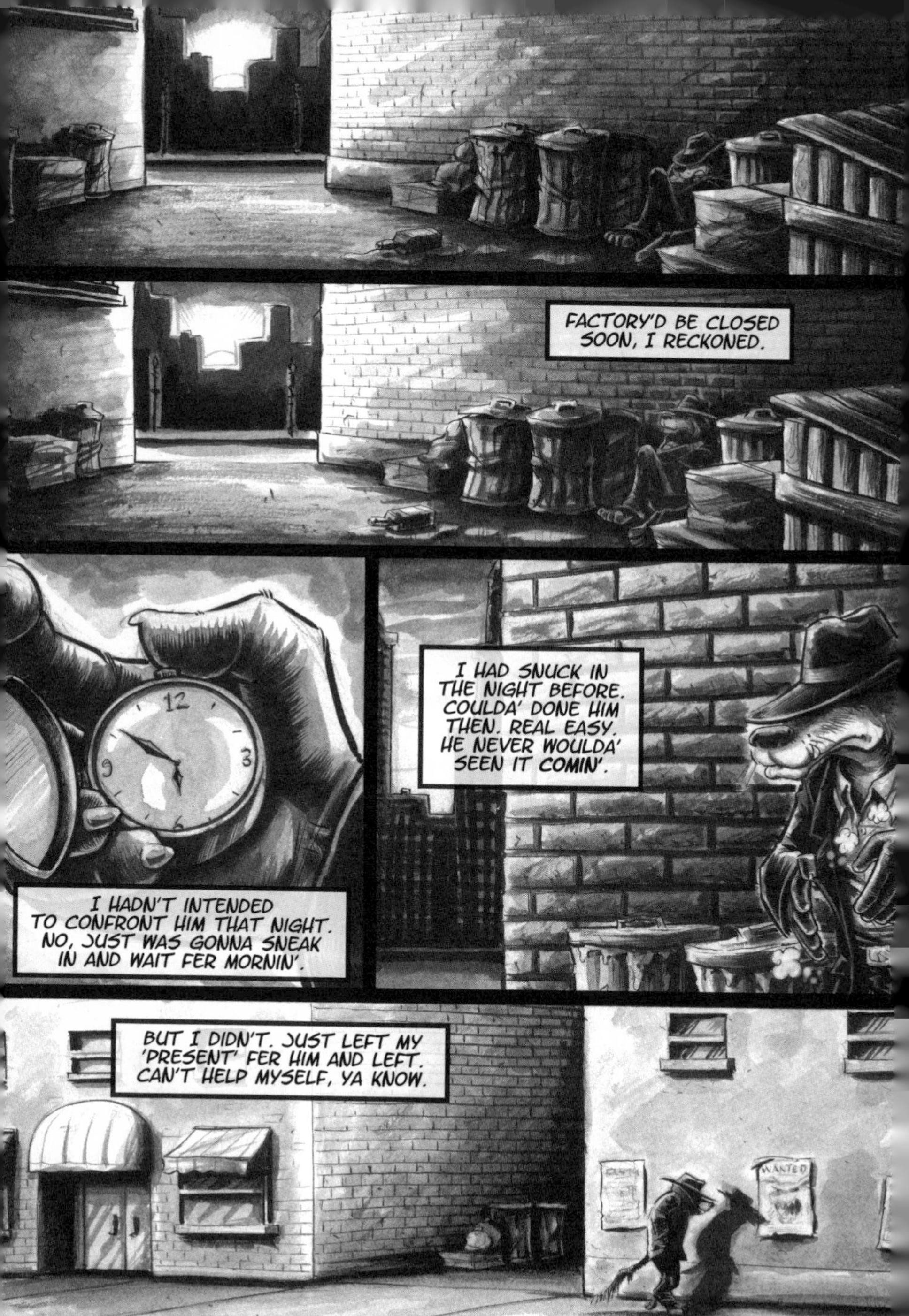
FACTORY'D BE CLOSED SOON, I RECKONED.
I HADN'T INTENDED TO CONFRONT HIM THAT NIGHT. NO, JUST WAS GONNA SNEAK IN AND WAIT FER MORNIN'.
I HAD SNUCK IN THE NIGHT BEFORE. COULDA' DONE HIM THEN. REAL EASY. HE NEVER WOULDA' SEEN IT COMIN'.
BUT I DIDN'T. JUST LEFT MY 'PRESENT' FER HIM AND LEFT. CAN'T HELP MYSELF, YA KNOW.
WANTED
I'M A MUSICIAN AFTER ALL. GOTS A FLAIR FER THE DRAMATIC.

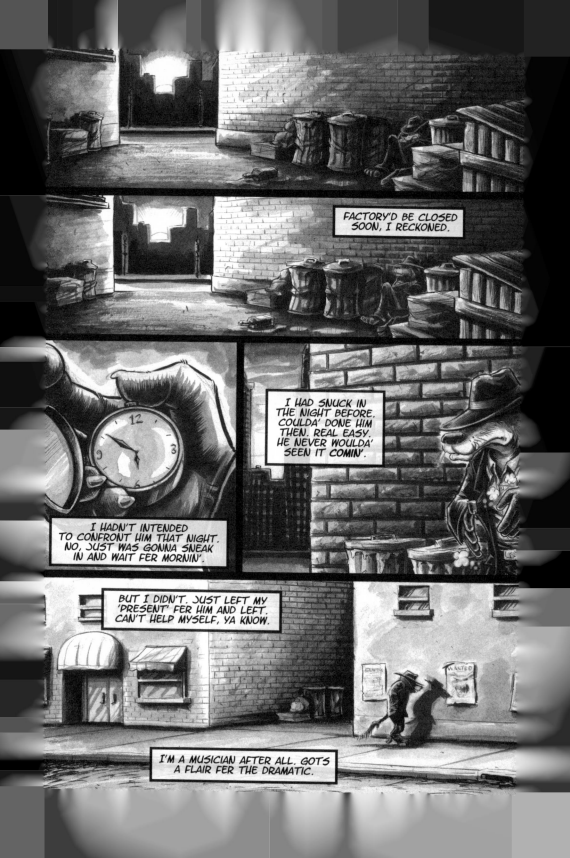

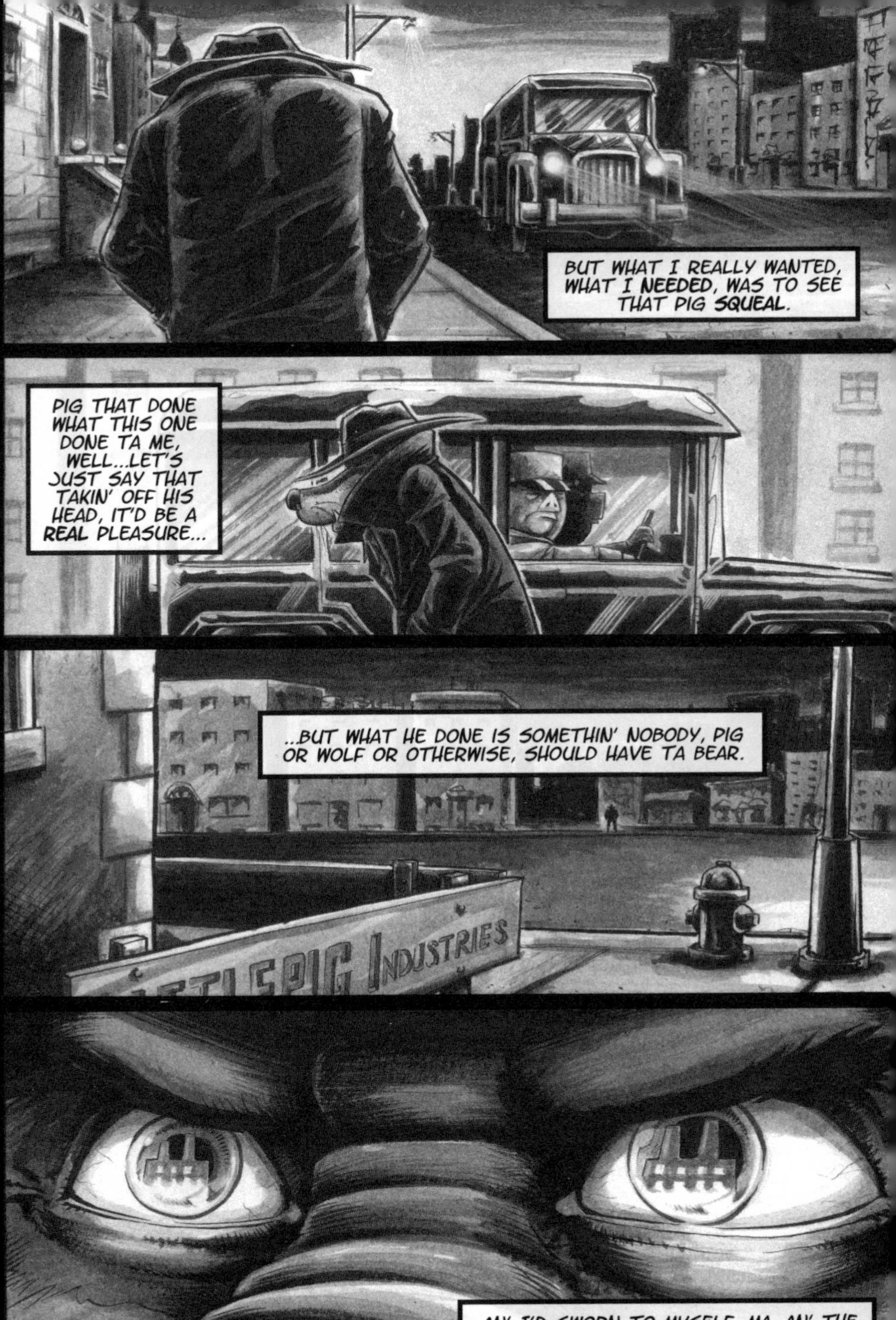
BUT WHAT I REALLY WANTED, WHAT I NEEDED, WAS TO SEE THAT PIG SQUEAL.
PIG THAT DONE WHAT THIS ONE DONE TA ME, WELL...LET'S JUST SAY THAT TAKIN' OFF HIS HEAD, IT'D BE A REAL PLEASURE...
...BUT WHAT HE DONE IS SOMETHIN' NOBODY, PIG OR WOLF OR OTHERWISE, SHOULD HAVE TA BEAR.
INDUSTRIES
AN' I'D SWORN TO MYSELF, MA, AN' THE CUBS THAT I'D SEE HIM SUFFER FOR IT.

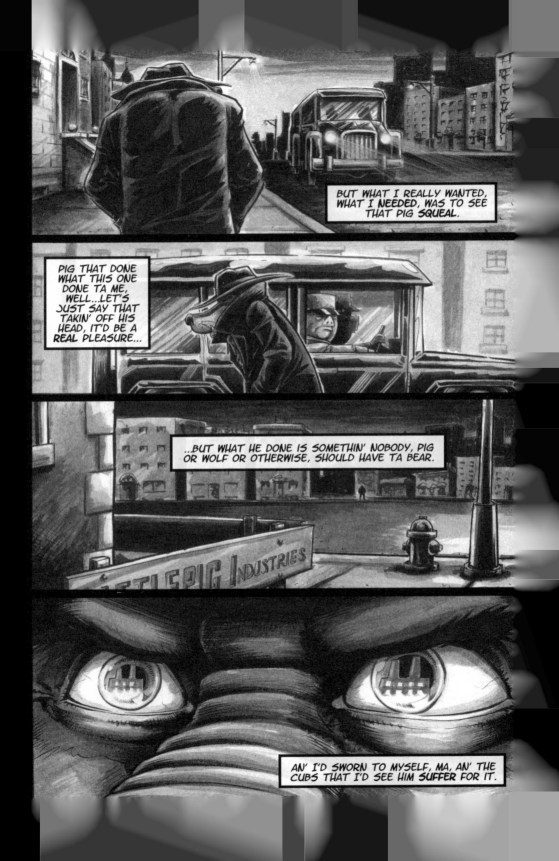

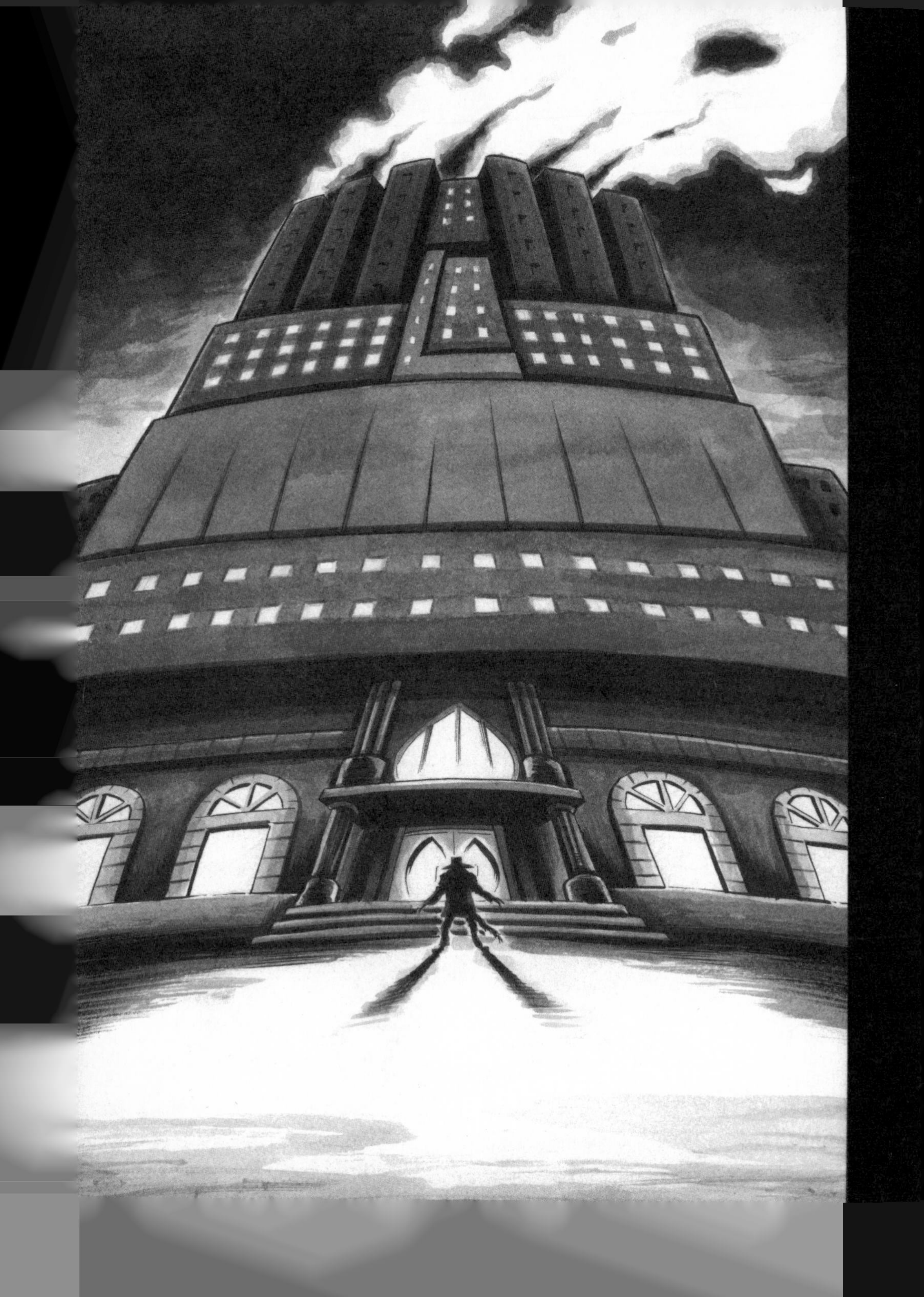

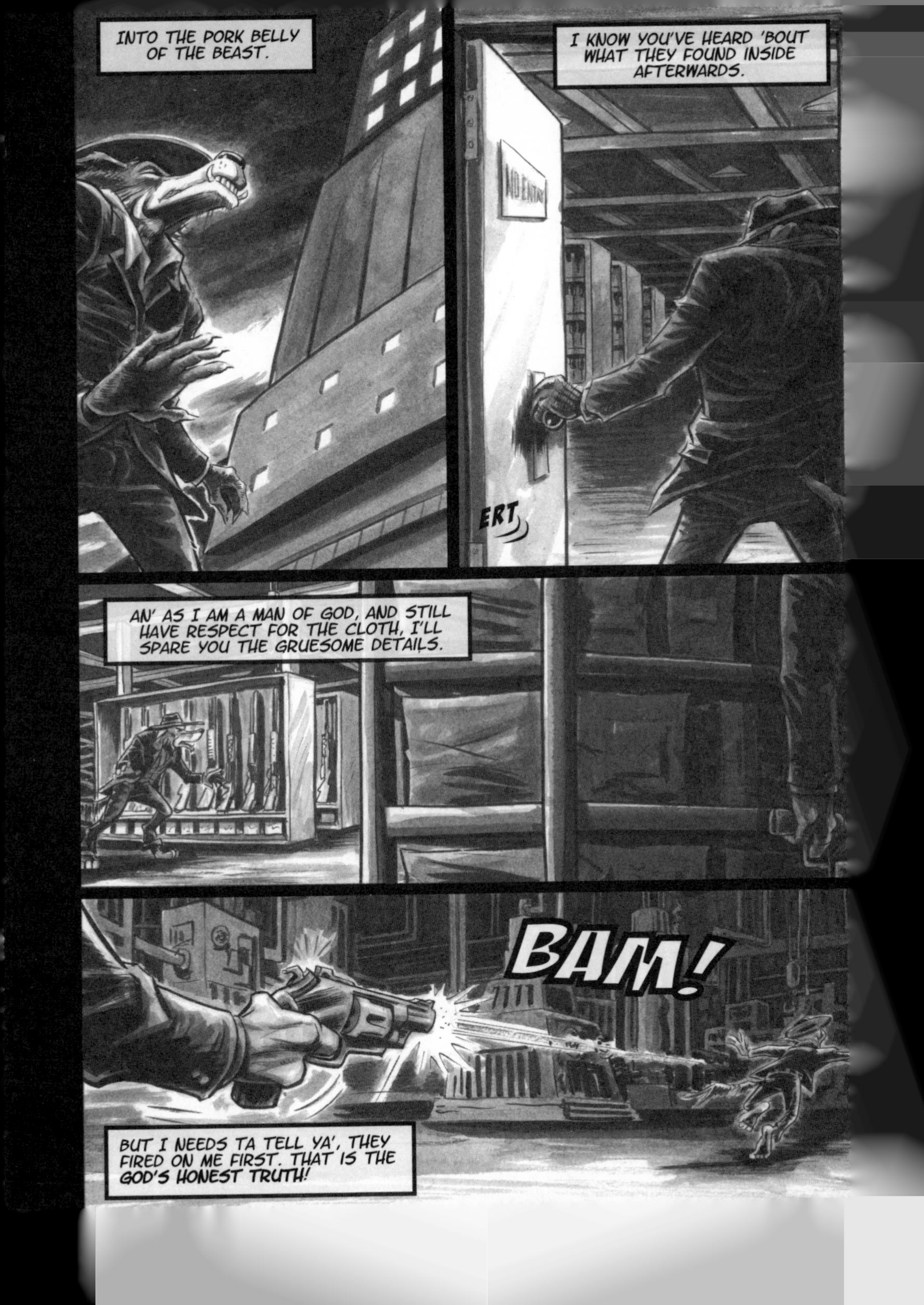
INTO THE PORK BELLY OF THE BEAST.
I KNOW YOU'VE HEARD 'BOUT WHAT THEY FOUND INSIDE AFTERWARDS.
NO ENTRY
ERT
AN' AS I AM A MAN OF GOD, AND STILL HAVE RESPECT FOR THE CLOTH, I'LL SPARE YOU THE GRUESOME DETAILS.
BAM!
BUT I NEEDS TA TELL YA', THEY FIRED ON ME FIRST. THAT IS THE GOD'S HONEST TRUTH!

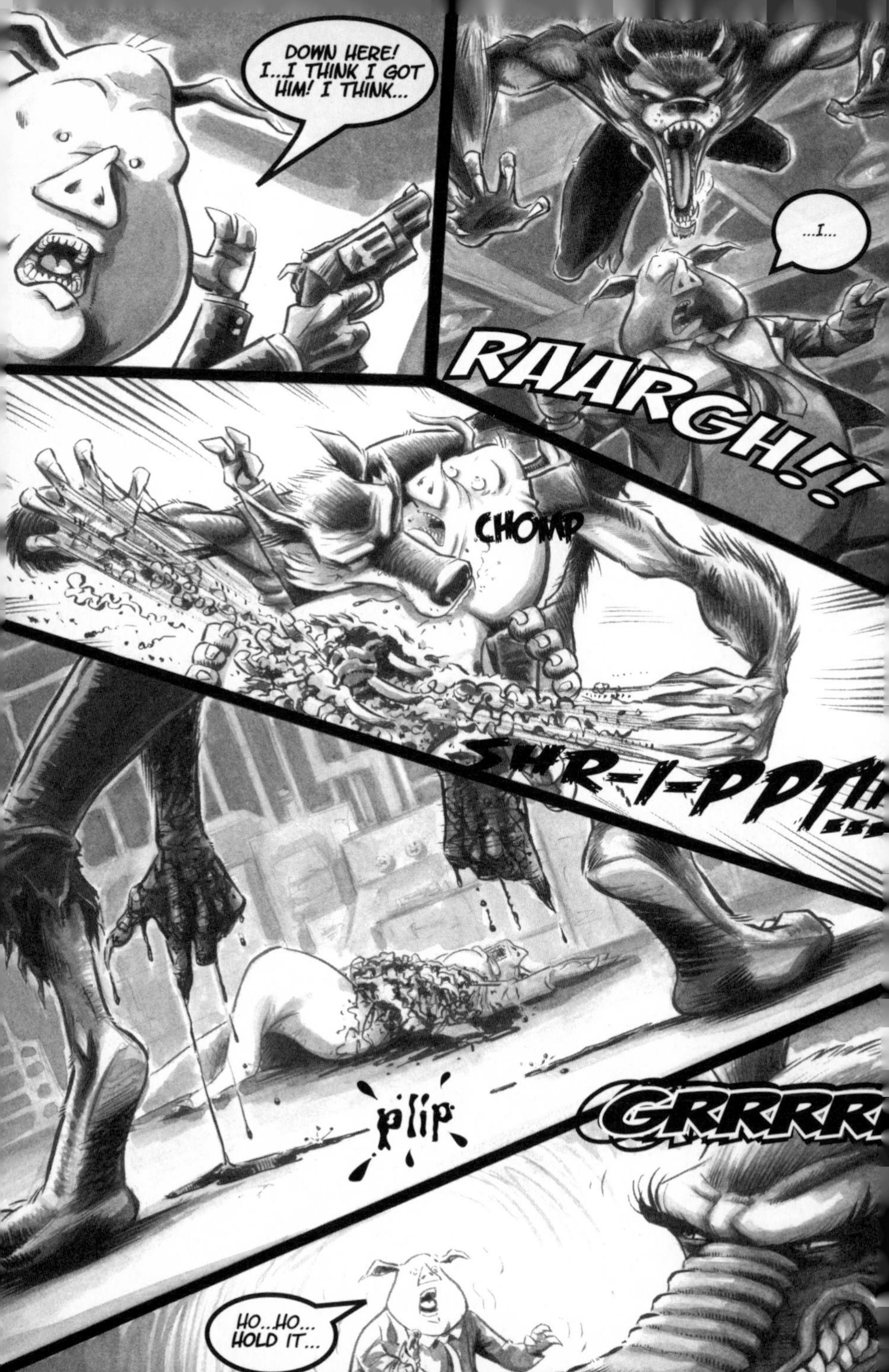

DOWN HERE! I...I THINK I GOT HIM! I THINK...
...I...
RAARGH!!!
CHOMP
SHR-I-PPT!!!
plip
GRRRR
HO...HO... HOLD IT...

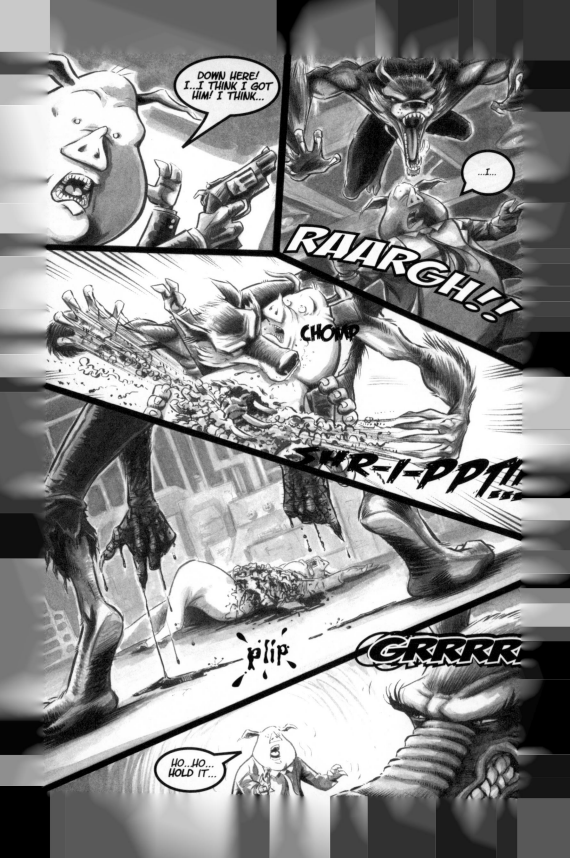

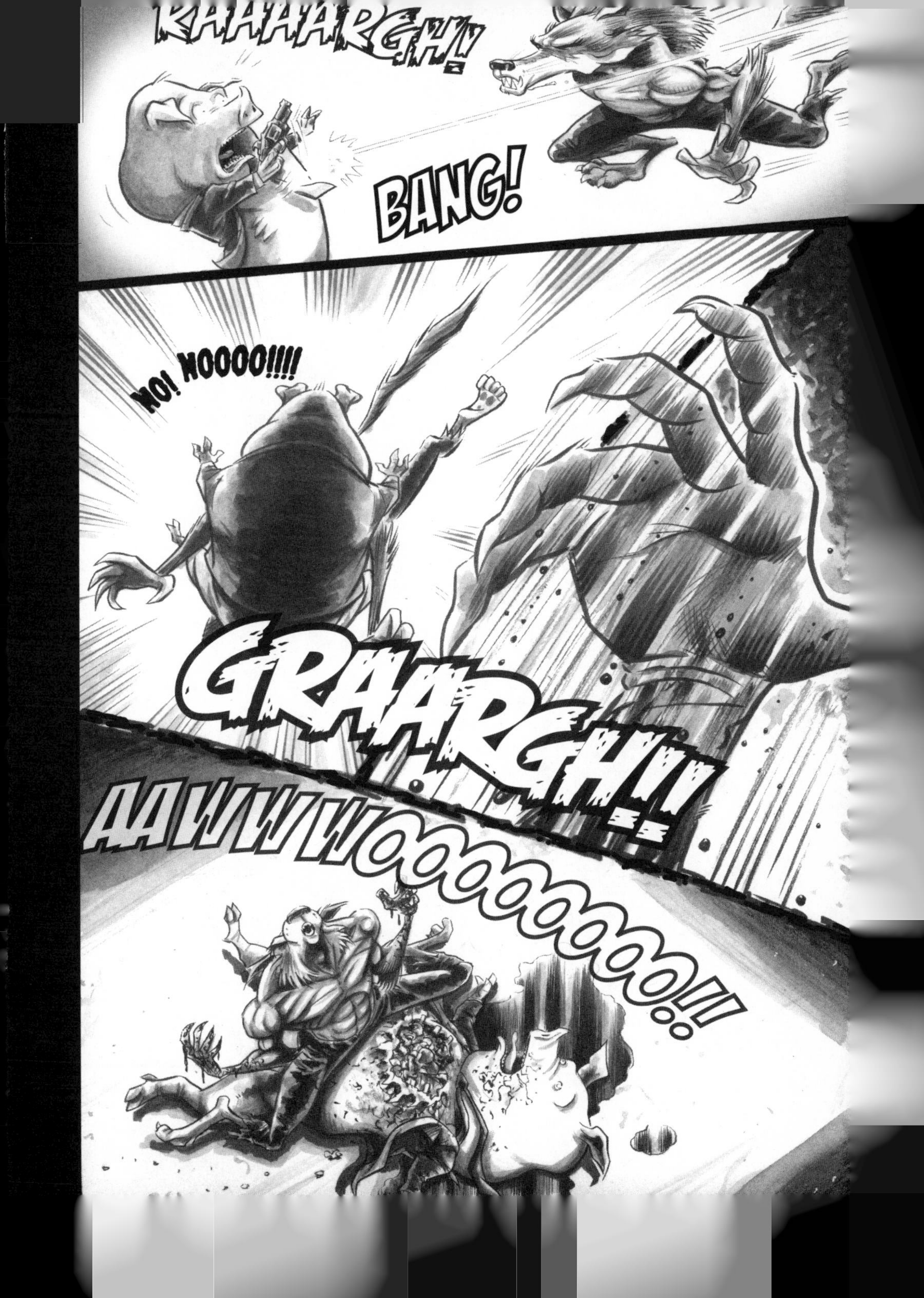

KAAAARGH!!
BANG!
NO! NOOOO!!!!
GRAARGH!!
AAWWWOOOOOOOOOO!!!

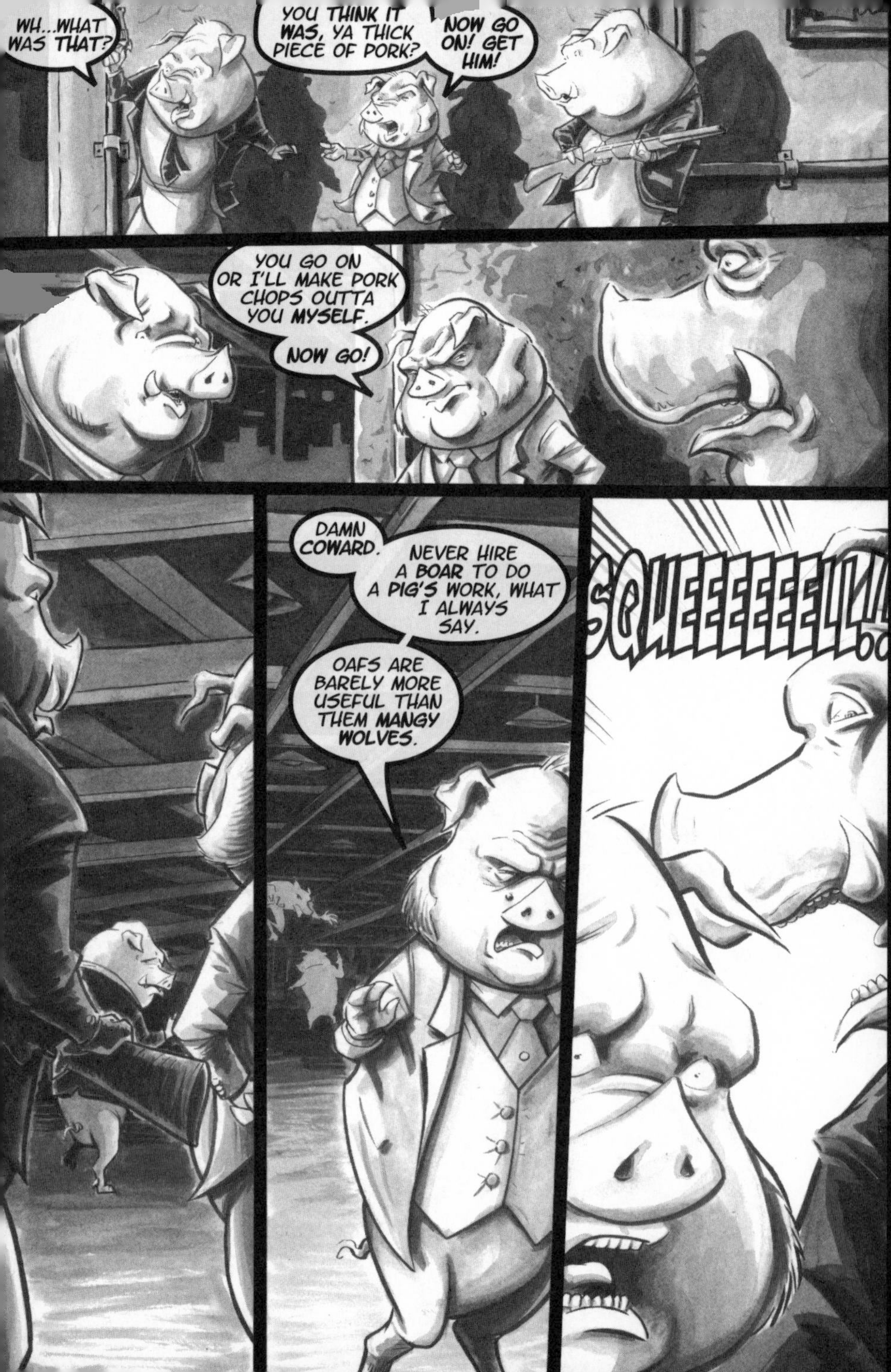
WH...WHAT WAS THAT?
YOU THINK IT WAS, YA THICK PIECE OF PORK?
NOW GO ON! GET HIM!
YOU GO ON OR I'LL MAKE PORK CHOPS OUTTA YOU MYSELF.
NOW GO!
DAMN COWARD.
NEVER HIRE A BOAR TO DO A PIG'S WORK, WHAT I ALWAYS SAY.
OAFS ARE BARELY MORE USEFUL THAN THEM MANGY WOLVES.
SQUEEEEEEELL

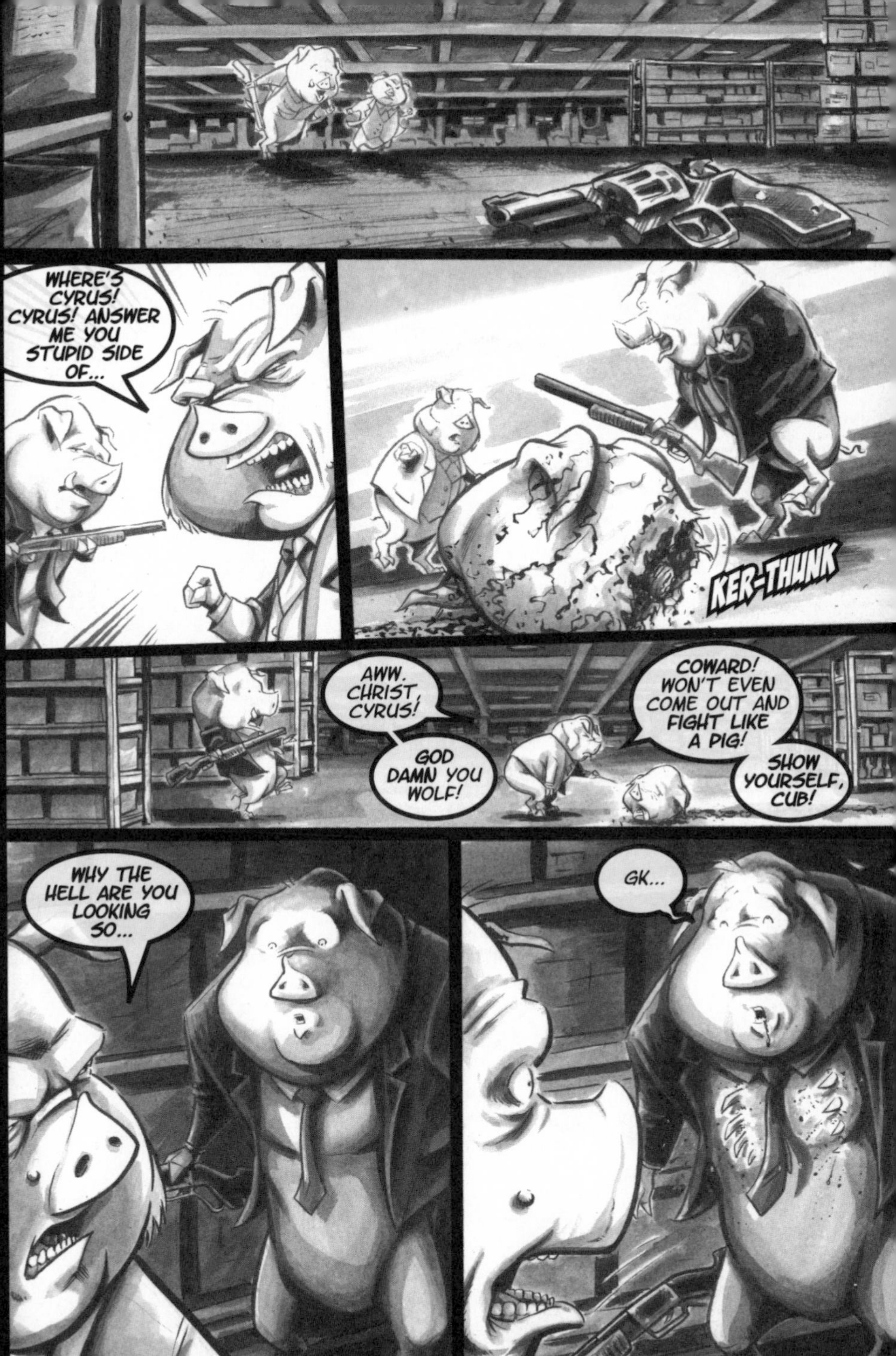
WHERE'S CYRUS! CYRUS! ANSWER ME YOU STUPID SIDE OF...
KER-THUNK
AWW. CHRIST, CYRUS!
GOD DAMN YOU WOLF!
COWARD! WON'T EVEN COME OUT AND FIGHT LIKE A PIG!
SHOW YOURSELF, CUB!
WHY THE HELL ARE YOU LOOKING SO...
GK...

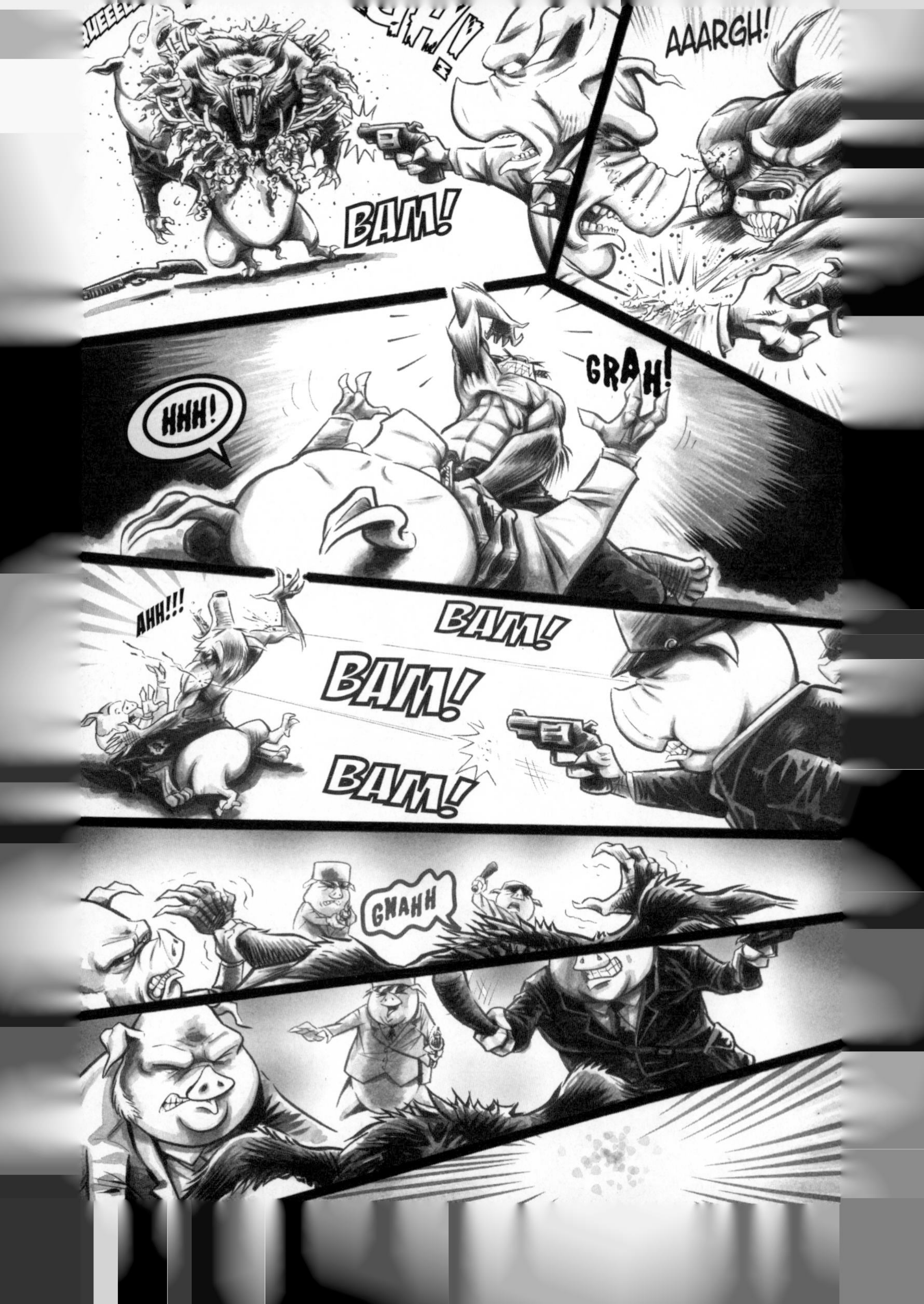
BAM!
AAARGH!
GRAH!
HHH!
AHH!!!
BAM!
BAM!
BAM!
GNAHH

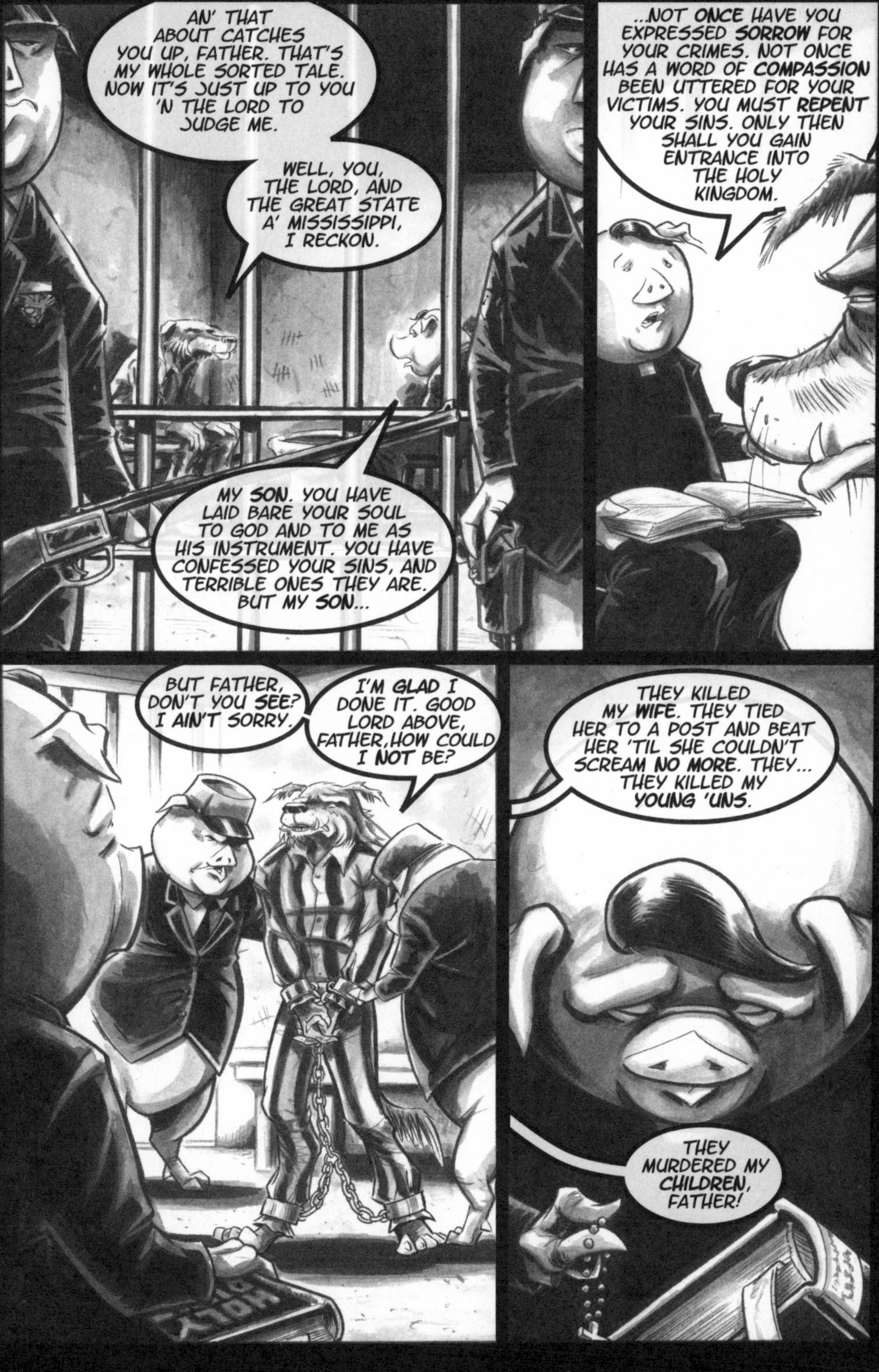
AN' THAT ABOUT CATCHES YOU UP, FATHER. THAT'S MY WHOLE SORTED TALE. NOW IT'S JUST UP TO YOU 'N THE LORD TO JUDGE ME.
WELL, YOU, THE LORD, AND THE GREAT STATE A' MISSISSIPPI, I RECKON.
MY SON. YOU HAVE LAID BARE YOUR SOUL TO GOD AND TO ME AS HIS INSTRUMENT. YOU HAVE CONFESSED YOUR SINS, AND TERRIBLE ONES THEY ARE. BUT MY SON...
...NOT ONCE HAVE YOU EXPRESSED SORROW FOR YOUR CRIMES. NOT ONCE HAS A WORD OF COMPASSION BEEN UTTERED FOR YOUR VICTIMS. YOU MUST REPENT YOUR SINS. ONLY THEN SHALL YOU GAIN ENTRANCE INTO THE HOLY KINGDOM.
BUT FATHER, DON'T YOU SEE? I AIN'T SORRY.
I'M GLAD I DONE IT. GOOD LORD ABOVE, FATHER, HOW COULD I NOT BE?
THEY KILLED MY WIFE. THEY TIED HER TO A POST AND BEAT HER 'TIL SHE COULDN'T SCREAM NO MORE. THEY... THEY KILLED MY YOUNG 'UNS.
THEY MURDERED MY CHILDREN, FATHER!

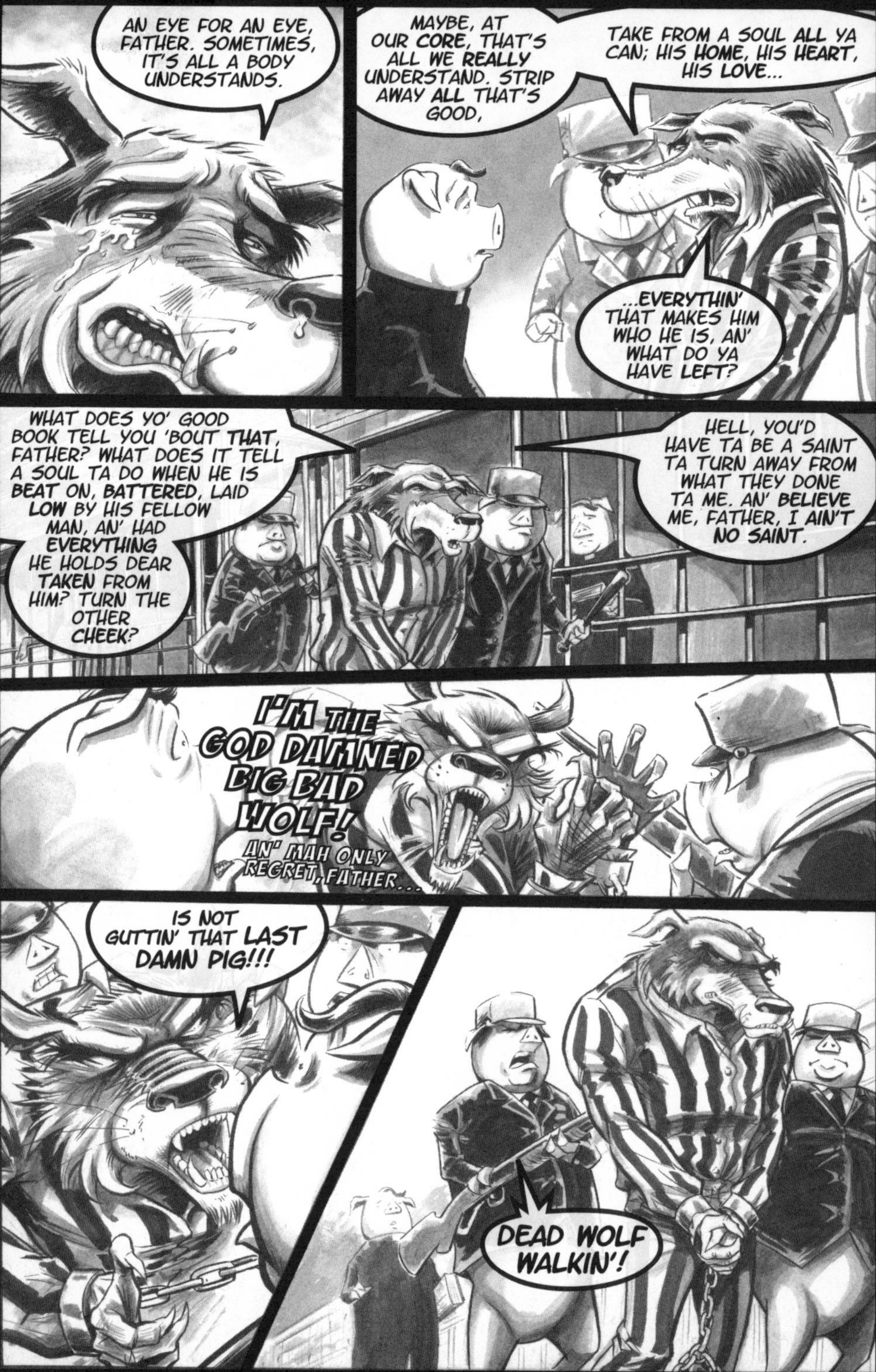
AN EYE FOR AN EYE, FATHER. SOMETIMES, IT'S ALL A BODY UNDERSTANDS.
MAYBE, AT OUR CORE, THAT'S ALL WE REALLY UNDERSTAND. STRIP AWAY ALL THAT'S GOOD,
TAKE FROM A SOUL ALL YA CAN; HIS HOME, HIS HEART, HIS LOVE...
...EVERYTHIN' THAT MAKES HIM WHO HE IS, AN' WHAT DO YA HAVE LEFT?
WHAT DOES YO' GOOD BOOK TELL YOU 'BOUT THAT, FATHER? WHAT DOES IT TELL A SOUL TA DO WHEN HE IS BEAT ON, BATTERED, LAID LOW BY HIS FELLOW MAN, AN' HAD EVERYTHING HE HOLDS DEAR TAKEN FROM HIM? TURN THE OTHER CHEEK?
HELL, YOU'D HAVE TA BE A SAINT TA TURN AWAY FROM WHAT THEY DONE TA ME. AN' BELIEVE ME, FATHER, I AIN'T NO SAINT.
I'M THE GOD DAMNED BIG BAD WOLF!
AN' MAH ONLY REGRET, FATHER...
IS NOT GUTTIN' THAT LAST DAMN PIG!!!
DEAD WOLF WALKIN'!

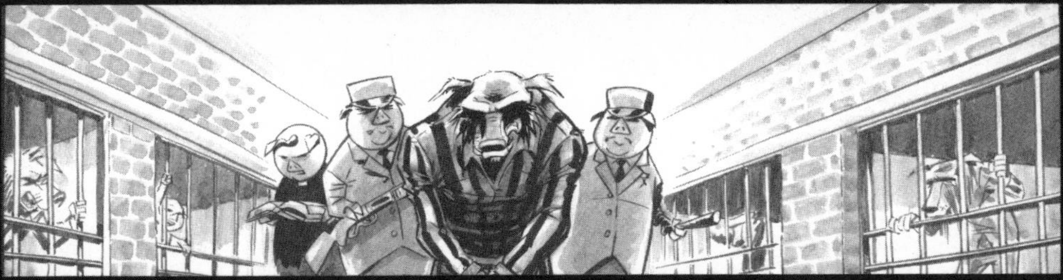

From the Clarion-Ledger, Jackson, MS. October 13th, 1920.

A reign of terror has ended and the survivors of the victims can rest easier now as convicted murderer BB Wolf was put to death today at the Choctaw County Prison.

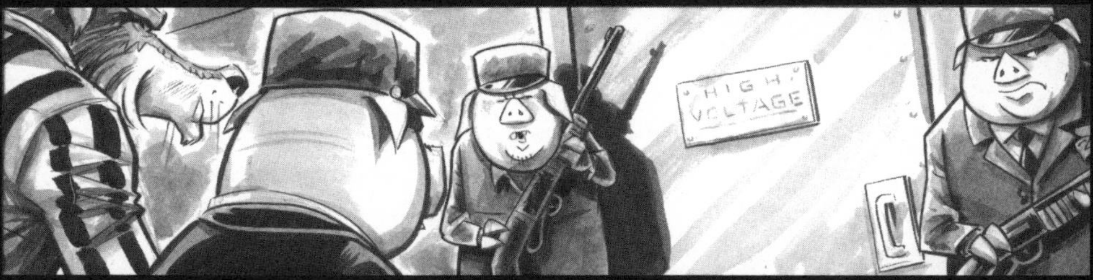
HIGH VOLTAGE

Though Mr. Wolf's killing spree extended past the borders of the great state of Mississippi, spilling over into our northern neighbors of Missouri and Illinois, it was here the killing began and here where most of his victims fell.

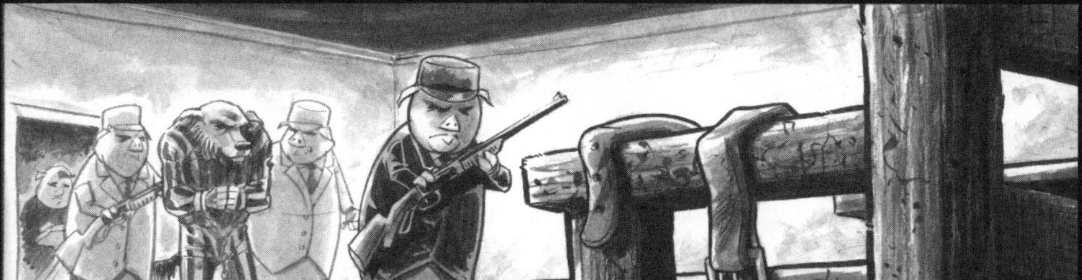

Jurors, judges, and lawyers alike sat stunned and horrified as they learned of the unthinkable deeds done by Mr. Wolf during his four-week, mass murdering rampage.

The brutal slaughters of prominent businessmen Alouissius Littlepig of Money, Mississippi and his elder brother, Beauregard Littlepig of East St. Louis, seemed to set the stage for a classic tale of murderous revenge against a family that, Mr. Wolf maintained, had wronged him.

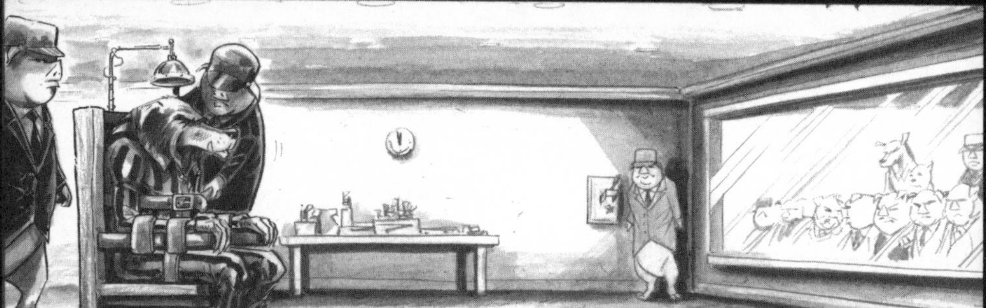

But it was Mr. Wolf's unfathomable murdering of his wife, six young cubs, and the subsequent slaughter of nearly twenty more poor souls throughout the surrounding farming communities of Money that convinced jurors to seek the death penalty in this case.

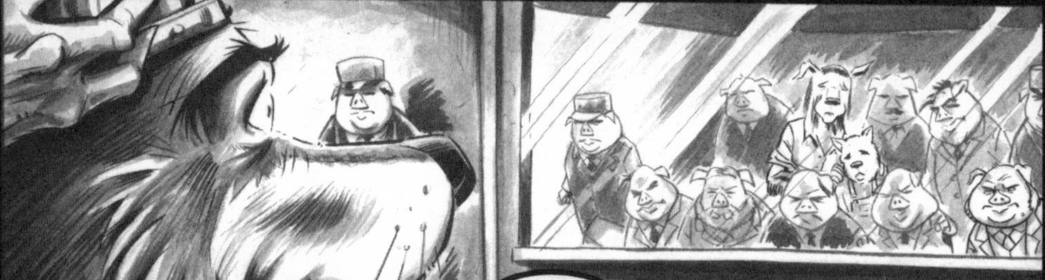
REMY?

And, in a twist that is found only in the pulps, it was the eldest brother of the two slain Littlepigs, northern industrialist Carrington Littlepig, who aided police in the capture of this brazen, maniacal killer.

Led by his own twisted vision of revenge, BB Wolf stormed the Chicago-based processing plant of Littlepig Industries with the obvious intention of murdering the elder Littlepig.

Only through his own cunning, and the aide of police, was Mr. Littlepig able to finally bring Mr. Wolf to justice.

And so here, in Choctaw County, at precisely 12:00 A.M. on the 13th of October, 1920, the switch was thrown and the lights put out on this state's most notorious mass murderer.

Dozens, perhaps hundreds, of wolves camped outside the prison all day and night showing surprising support for and declaring the innocence of Mr. Wolf in the charges of the slain farmers of Money. But even they, in the face of such compelling testimony from respected business pigs and associates of the slain, must accept the decision handed down.

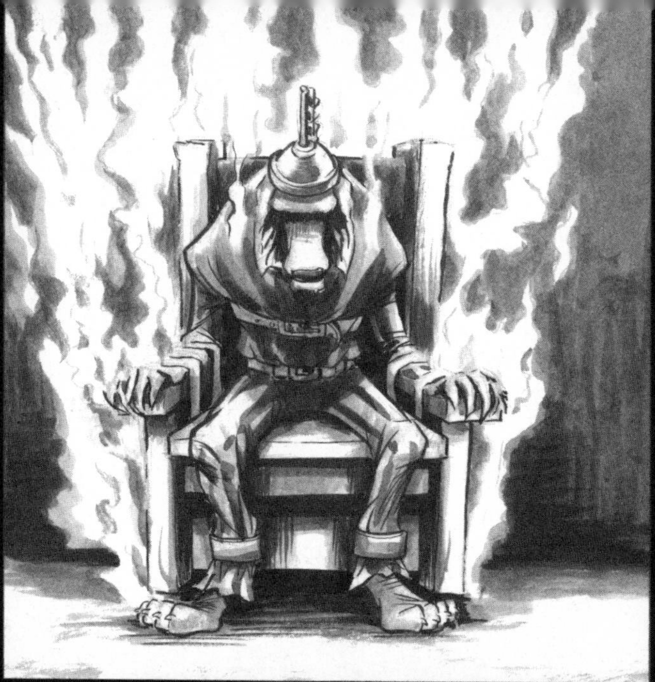

One can only hope that this will bring some measure of peace to those touched by this monster's bloody rampage and that this sad chapter of horror and death has finally come to an end.

One can only hope.

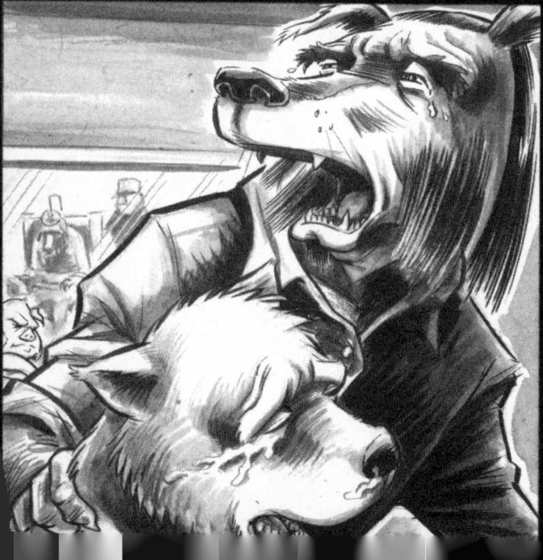

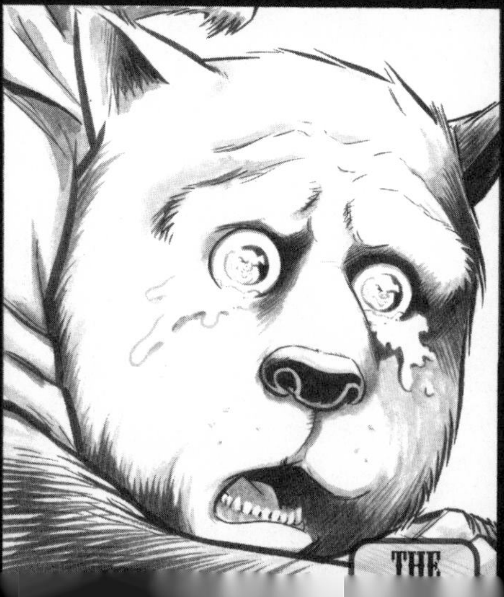
THE

Acknowledgements:

I would like to extend my heartfelt thanks to all involved in realizing this dream, from Rich, CJ, Chrissy and Tony, to Brett, Chris, Rob and Leigh. Ryan, thank you for your continued support and for getting the book in front of you-know-who. Troy, thank you for your superb design work. Austin & Jesse...you know why. And lastly, but most importantly, thank you Katie and Charlotte. You are my inspiration, my reason for being, my light and my life. I do this all for you.

—JD

Thanks to Johnnie and Katie for thinking of me when they were looking for an artist for BB. Working with them was an extremely enjoyable and rewarding process, but the greatest reward was making two new friends. Also, thanks must go out to my "go-to guy" CJ Bettin and his fantastic assistant Chrissy for swooping in and fixing up the lettering files for us. CJ always comes through for me and is the best friend anyone could hope for. Finally, thanks, as always, to my wife Sandy and my daughter Stella. Support and strength!

—Rich

BB Wolf & The Howlers
– Afterword by JD Arnold

History, they say, is written by the victorious. An adage as old as written history perhaps, and one written, most certainly, by the same said victorious. And if taken as gospel, the wise and cynical man can, rightfully so, posit an inherent dishonesty in the supposed historical facts this adage speaks of. It would seem reasonable to assume a measure of prejudice in the recounting of one's own deeds, especially when setting them down to the printed page for the purposes of posterity, for the very pointed purpose of creating one's own immortality. And in truth it has become common for the modern scholar to question that which was once unquestioned, what was once accepted as gospel. The search for truth is nothing if not relentless. Through advancements in the fields of medicine, archaeology, and forensics, just to name a few, we have seen not only our world, and the perception of our world, change, but we have seen history literally rewritten. It has come to pass that we know history as a fluid body, not 'written in stone' as we once believed. The times they are a-changin', my friends, and they are changing behind as well as ahead.

It was with this perspective that I began my journey of discovery into the American South of 1920, to the town of Money, Mississippi, and into the now infamous legend that is one BB Wolf. If you are reading these notes, if you hold in your hands the story that has, after so many lost years, come to see the light of day once again, then you've no doubt come to know, at the very least, the broad strokes of the truth. You've heard the *NPR* interviews, you've seen the *Dateline* expose. For those who have read the book, here is a recap of what had been, for far too long, held as truth. Barnabus Benjamin Wolf was born to James and Esther Wolf in Money, Mississippi in or around 1887. No official record of his birth has ever been uncovered, and only a rough estimation of his age at time of death gives us this date. Of his parents we know little, but records of land holdings exist among many from the years of Reconstruction, and from these we were able to begin to piece together a family history. Further, a land deed in the name of one Barnabus Benjamin and Eleanor Kate Wolf, willed by one Romulus T. Lupine, was found in the Leflore County Archives. But only these two facts remain, a small testament to the life of BB Wolf and his family. These two only, that is, until the well, if not accurately, documented events of 1920. We all know the story: a tale of misguided rage, unspeakable murder, and the eventual fall of a lost and tortured soul. Nearly a dozen deaths were attributed to the hands of BB Wolf, a seemingly simple and unassuming farmer and family man. Worse, among the murdered were his wife and children. Many could not fathom the direness of his actions, the depravity of a mind capable of such dastardly deeds. But the facts seemed to speak against him and, despite the protestations from many of BB's neighbors and surviving family, Mr. Wolf was found to be wanting by a jury of his 'peers', and put to death by electrocution late in the summer of 1920. For most this put to rest a dark nightmare.

Justice, it seemed, had been served. And for those for whom justice had certainly miscarried, well, it is simply said that the cards were stacked squarely against them. The same system that had brought BB to a swift, if not righteous, justice, would also ensure the silencing of any dissenting voice to the contrary. Right or wrong, the life of BB Wolf had come to an end. And as the victors wrote, it was most certainly right.

And so it was written, and so the world believed. The legend of BB Wolf, murderer, was born. And lost was the truth of who BB Wolf was, and the influence he had on the early, formative years of the American Blues movement.

BB Wolf was a pioneer in the style that would become known as the Mississippi Delta Blues. Though many contest the presence of any substantial differences in music originating in the region, the characteristics commonly sited — the use of a bottleneck slide, and the emphasis on rhythm, the wailing harmonica and soulful vocals — are certainly heard in those early recordings. With the discovery of the lost tracks, recorded nearly a decade before the first major recording of a Delta Blues artist, the influence BB Wolf had on such Blues greats as Big Dog Williams, Garfield Barkers, Willie Browncoat, Snoopy Pryor, Hound Dog Taylor, and Howlin' Wolf (no known relation) is clearly seen.

One can only speculate the further contributions he could have made to the form. His body of work is but a handful of songs contained in those recordings, but his legend is now immense, and his life, for many, finally vindicated. Through research into the lost blues legend, I have uncovered never-before-seen letters leading me to BB's descendants, one surviving grandson and many great-grandchildren. Interviews with his family, supported by documents retrieved from the Leflore County Archives have led me to believe in the innocence of BB Wolf. Further details and my complete notes pertaining to the false conviction of BB Wolf can be found in my book The Delta Runs Red. But I do feel it necessary to thank BB's grandson, Clifford J. Wolf, the director of the Leflore County Historical Society, Margaret Bowers, and documentarian Kenneth Bacon, among so many others, for their invaluable assistance in my research.

I also need to thank the blues community within this country. They are too numerous to list, but have been nothing but willing to finally bring the truth of BB Wolf to light. His life had become a fable, an oral tradition passed down through generations. A tale told and kept alive in the bars, juke joints, and blues clubs scattered across this land. Born of truth but believed by most now to be a parable, a metaphor to the all-too-familiar struggle of the wolf. And powerful as the metaphor can be, the community, the world, has gained something ever more profound. The Truth. The peace this has brought to the family of Mr. Wolf is immeasurable. The importance it holds to the family of Bluesmen who carry his legacy will surely come to light in the coming years. The courts of Leflore County have yet to overturn what was certainly a false verdict, condemning an innocent wolf to death in the summer of 1920. We can only hope this final act of vindication comes in our lifetime.

Reprinted here for the first time are the handwritten lyrics to the only three recordings known to exist by legendary Bluesman, BB Wolf. Lyrics provided courtesy of Clifford J. Wolf.

Sweet Baby Elle

There Aint no woman Finer
Than my sweet Baby Elle
I said There Aint no woman Finer
Than my sweet Baby Elle
Got no need to look ~~for another~~ Further
No reason I can tell
Cuz There Aint no woman love me like my Elle do
No There Aint no woman can love my like my Elle do
Love me all day long Lord
Love me the ~~wto~~ whole night ~~through~~
Let me tell all you Fellas keep yo paws ~~get off~~ my wife
Yep I warnin you Fellas keep yo paws from my wife
See she a one man woman
Make the other men Fear for their life
Yep she a one man woman and don't you know I am that man
A one man woman Lord know I am that man
~~Man~~ keep me high and happy Lord
Love me like no one else can
She keep me warm on a winter night cool on a summer day
make me wet when I am dry Lord bring me home when I stray
Aint no other woman love me hard like Elle do
Love me so nice when I'm good Lord Love me when I'd bad to
Cuz she my sweet Fine woman
My sweet Baby Elle
She'll lead me to your Holy gates Lord
And she'd Follow me through Hell

Freight Train

Freight Train
Takes my beat blues on down the line
Freight Train rollin
Take my poor heart down the line
Cant live here in this darkness
Got to leave my pain behind

Cuz 1 done lost
Done lost all 1 ever had
Lost my heart and my home Lord
Lost so much it drive me mad
And to bring it all on back now
No Wolf has ever been so bad
The pigs done took away
Everything that made me me
Took all 1 ever was
All 1 was ever meant to be
Now all 1 got inside
Is a heart that beat so black
Gonna hear them pigs a squeelin
When this Big Bad Wolf attacks
But til then Freight Train
Take my blues on down the line
Cant live here in this
Got to leave my pain behind

RIP IT UP

Well I'm gonna rip it up
I'm gonna Tear it down
I'm gonna huff I'm gonna puff
I'm gonna Tear This here house right on down to The ground
Whiskey an blues They my medicine
Help heal alla lifes little scars
But some a them cuts Theys a little to deep
Booze an blues only Take you so far
Yeah I'm gonna rip it up yeah I'm gonna Tear it down
I'm gonna huff I'm gonna puff
An I'm gonna Tear This here house right on down to the ground
Well I got my house in order
Work hard build it up mind my own
But a house just a house If it just wood n nails
Filled with a familys what make it a home
Yeah rip it up Yeah Tear it down
I'm gonna huff an I'm gonna puff
I'm gonna Tear This here house right on down To The ground
See but not all homes made a wood or brick
Most of em made outta Straw
All I got but They gone and Take it away
well I aint gonna live by no Little pig law
I'm gonna rip them then up I'm gonna Tear them down
I'm gonna Huff and I'm gonna puff
An I'm gonna Tear Them pig house
right on down To The ever lovin ground

Barnabus B. Wolf,
Mississippi State Penitentiary,
October 3rd, 1920

BB Wolf, 1916.

BB Wolf and The Howlers, 1919.
From left to right,
Rufus Shanks, BB Wolf,
Collier 'Droop' Washington.

PPP rally, Summer 1919, location unknown. Pictured, front row, left to right:
Francis Mayer, Beauregard Littlepig, Carrington Littlepig, Alouissius Littlepig.

About the authors:

JD Arnold opened the pages of his first comic book some 38 years ago and has not been heard from since. In the spring of 2007 he realized a life-long dream by becoming a co-owner in his local comical book selling shop, Comicopolis. This year another dream comes true with the release of his first professionally published graphic novel. He hopes to continue a life of meager wages by writing and selling these four-color gems well into his eighties, or until the state lottery sees fit to pull his numbers! C'mon! He currently lives in Santa Cruz, CA. with his lovely wife Katie and beautiful, but ravenous, daughter Charlotte.

Rich Koslowski is best known for his fan friendly comic book series *The 3 Geeks* (later *Geeksville*), the recipient of three Eisner Award nominations. He also wrote and illustrated the much-lauded graphic novel *Three Fingers* in 2002 (published by Top Shelf Productions), which won the coveted Ignatz Award for Outstanding Graphic Novel and was named as one of the 500 Essential Graphic Novels in 2008. In 2005 his second graphic novel with Top Shelf, *The King*, was released. In 2007 he wrote his first novel, *The List*. 2008 brought Rich his first writing assignment for Marvel Comics, rebooting their popular Guardian character, now named Weapon Omega. To view Rich's works visit his website at RichKoslowski.com